101 WAYS TO WIN
IN TEACHING IN SECONDARY SCHOOL

Managing Behaviour, Workload and Wellbeing

Gurdeep Singh

PUBLISHER'S INFORMATION

We hope you find the ideas in this book helpful. Brilliant Publications publishes many other books to support teachers. To find out more details on any of our titles, please go to our website: www.brilliantpublications.co.uk.

Published by Brilliant Publications Limited
Unit 10
Sparrow Hall Farm
Edlesborough
Dunstable
Bedfordshire
LU6 2ES, UK

E-mail: customer-services@brilliantpublications.co.uk

www.brilliantpublications.co.uk

Brilliant Publications is a registered trademark.

Written by Gurdeep Singh
Illustrated by Elisa Rocchi
Cover designed by Brilliant Publications Limited
Bottom left cover photo: Aylesbury Grammar School. All other cover photos, Shutterstock. Photo contributors: Robert Kneschke, Johner Images and Monkey Business Images
Inside pages designed by emc Design

© Brilliant Publications Limited 2024

printed: ISBN 978-1-78317-354-9
pdf: ISBN 978-1-78317-355-6

First printed and published in 2024

The right of Gurdeep Singh to be identified as the author of this work has been asserted by himself in accordance with the Copyright, Designs and Patents Act 1988.

All rights reserved. Apart from any use permitted under UK copyright law, no part of this publication may be reproduced or transmitted in any form or by any means, electronic or mechanical, including photocopying and recording, or held within any information storage and retrieval system, without permission in writing from the publishers or under licence from the Copyright Licensing Agency Limited. Further details of such licenses (for reprographic reproduction) may be obtained from the Copyright Licensing Agency Limited, 5th Floor, Shackleton House, 4 Battle Bridge Lane, London SE1 2HX (https://cla.co.uk).

CONTENTS

INTRODUCTION 7

CHAPTER 1 THE STARTER 8–28

CHAPTER 2 BEST OF THE BEST 29–52

1. Thank you, it has been a pleasure 30
2. Let the good kids win 31
3. Really make them think at the start of the lesson 32
4. Stock balls and doosras 33
5. Replace the word 'work' with 'learning' 34
6. Find out about the best teachers in your school and ask yourself why 35
7. Accept that it will take time (and focus on the positives) 36
8. Hands-down questioning 37
9. Stand up, sit down 39
10. Be a great form tutor 40
11. A laugh and a smile? Rudeness and disrespect or just embarrassment? 41
12. Make confrontations a win-win 41
13. Simplicity of a three-part lesson 43
14. Anagrams – to asrtt and ifshin 43
15. Bad lessons? Blame yourself first 44
16. Slay the marking monster – who is working harder? 15-minute challenge 45
17. Slay the planning monster – 10-minute preparation 46
18. Support circles – learn from others 47
19. Support staff – the heart and body of the school 48
20. Wellbeing – YOU have the power to change the way you view things 49
21. Simple messages and instructions repeated over and over 50
22. Organisation – growing extra arms and legs 51

KEY TAKEAWAYS 52

CHAPTER 3 **THE POWER STRUGGLE** 53–71

23 Your classroom, your rules – seating plan 54
24 A look to say it all 54
25 Open your door, close their window of opportunity 56
26 Loose control or lose control 56
27 Sticky note questions 57
28 Don't enjoy the honeymoon too much 58
29 No dead time in lessons 59
30 Change 'if you do, then I will' for poor conduct to 'because you have, now I will' for good behaviour 60
31 Class wars and bad groups 60
32 Elastic band – stretch and relax 62
33 Empathise during tellings-off, don't rant 63
34 The power of the start 64
35 The power of the plenary 64
36 Testing for behaviour 65
37 Don't encourage an audience 66
38 Give them space in lessons – they need it 67
39 Ownership of the line 67
40 Write the following down 68
41 De-escalate 69

KEY TAKEAWAYS 71

CHAPTER 4 **THE HUMAN TOUCH** 72–88

42 Build lessons around what they need and want (and tell them what they want if they don't know) 74
43 'Yes, Sir', 'Yes, Miss' and the disarming smile 75
44 Name that name 76
45 Good detentions 76
46 Praise for everyone 77
47 Give a little piece of your heart 78
48 'I haven't got a pen' 79
49 Calming of the mind 80
50 Excuse me, am I boring you? 81
51 The pat on the back 82

52	Getting it wrong and changing your mind	83
53	Am I doing a good job? What could I change?	84
54	Meet and greet	84
55	The new student	85
56	Parents – emails and phone calls	86
	KEY TAKEAWAYS	88

CHAPTER 5 **WALK THE WALK** 89–107

57	Dress as a role model	90
58	Good morning, good morning	90
59	Enjoy the classroom	91
60	Extracurricular, extra respect	92
61	Aspirational pitching	93
62	Walk the unfamiliar school	94
63	Don't speak – they'll know what you're asking and thinking	95
64	Play your personality	96
65	Embrace and learn from bad lessons – don't brush those experiences under the carpet	97
66	The great resources hoarder	98
67	Enjoy the small victories	99
68	Parents' evenings – how to manage them	99
69	Technology – knowing when and how to use it	101
70	Complaints about students – keep things in perspective	102
71	Supply cover – the nightmare dream teacher job	102
72	Reading, reading, reading	104
73	The one-hour, six-lesson planning challenge	105
74	Ensure that your classroom is an extension of you	106
	KEY TAKEAWAYS	107

CHAPTER 6 **TALK THE TALK** 108–125

75	The controlled shout	109
76	Learn to act – watch wrestling!	110
77	Learn to act – watch stand-up comedy	111
78	The third person in the room	112
79	Perfect your lines	113

80	Only pause for applause	115
81	Explanation or argument?	116
82	The quiet mouse	117
83	Buying yourself time	118
84	The ineffective angry teacher – remember the dream?	119
85	Breaking the silence	120
86	Tweaking your (high) expectations	121
87	Build up to negatives and positives	122
88	Distracting the negatives	123
89	Cold comebacks	124
	KEY TAKEAWAYS	125

CHAPTER 7 **MIND GAMES** 126–142

90	Tales of the unexpected	127
91	The line between confidence and arrogance	128
92	Sweet little lies	129
93	Use the force	130
94	Talk choices	131
95	Magic and mystery	132
96	Develop their memory, build their confidence	133
97	Be larger than life	135
98	Eyes-closed feedback	136
99	A routine that students love	138
100	Student-led learning	139
101	A picture to say a thousand words	140
	KEY TAKEAWAYS	142

CHAPTER 8 **FAILING, TO LEARN** 143–162

CHAPTER 9 **THE PLENARY – THE END OF THE BEGINNING** 163–165

INTRODUCTION

The best profession in the world

Teaching truly is the best profession in the world. It would be very easy to criticise me for saying this, considering I have not done anything else (other than menial student summer jobs) in my working life. But I owe so much to teaching. Over nearly 25 years, the profession has taken me from being a shy and sheltered young adult – so lacking in self-belief and so full of anxiety that I would avoid meeting new people or steer away from unknown situations – to someone who can act serious, disappointed and even a little scary sometimes. I'm someone who can speak in front of hundreds (students, staff or parents) or be put on the spot and respond confidently, with a smile on my face and genuinely enjoy the whole experience.

Teaching has been my rock when personal situations have dealt knockout blows. Teaching has lifted me even higher when the joys of life have swept me off my feet. I have met so many remarkable young people through teaching who have energised, inspired and motivated me, and so many excellent colleagues who have developed my skills, without even knowing they were doing it.

Don't get me wrong, the ride certainly has not been easy, I have made mistakes, struggled with behaviour of individuals and classes, failed in roles and misjudged situations (as you will read later). But I have never resented my choice to go into teaching and have never considered another path. Dreaming about winning the lottery and living in the sun with my feet up all day does not count!

CHAPTER 1 **THE STARTER**

My story – day zero

It's 1997, the first day of the autumn term, a day that I have been ruminating about for months with a mix of controlled excitement and rational fear. It's a little like the final seconds before you experience the thrilling rollercoaster: strapped in, with no escape.

I am getting ready to meet my tutor group for the very first time. The small ship of elation inside me has definitely been engulfed by the raging sea of nerves. Do I really want to be a teacher? A proper teacher? Not a student teacher (as we were called back then), always protected by the 'real' member of staff in the classroom, keeping a close eye as I tried to exert my false authority. The 'real' teacher, who seemed to do nothing, absolutely nothing except be present, to get the class quiet and focused. Am I a 'real' teacher now? I am not convinced, but of course it is too late to back out now.

The countdown is ending and the ride is about to start. I have never been in a classroom 'on my own' before and have no idea if I can really cut it – I am doubting myself more and more.

Imposter syndrome has been my companion throughout my time in teaching, as I had gone from being a classroom teacher, to having departmental responsibilities, then being a head of year and to becoming a senior leader, where my decisions and actions impact all 'stakeholders' in the school. Having spoken to other colleagues, it's clear that doubting our own abilities is a common feature of teachers at all levels and experiences – despite the self-confidence and assurance that we can exude.

Back to my first 'proper' day. I approach the door and walk in to see 30 Year 8 faces staring at me. Considering the predominantly white makeup of the staff and student body in the school, I am fairly sure that I am not what they expect as their new form tutor but, in my limited experience, young people are less likely to immediately judge on appearance. However, I also know that I only have a small window to create the right picture of me for them. What were all those

CHAPTER 1 **THE STARTER**

things that had been drummed into me about setting clear rules and expectations from the start? In the days and hours beforehand, I had rehearsed a few lines to clearly establish myself as a teacher who was not to be messed with, but right now my mind is a large, blank void. The classroom is deadly silent. It is now or never. 'Err, good morning Year 8, my name is, err, Mr Singh and I am your, err, new form tutor.'

The previous day, we'd had an inset day. I was publicly welcomed to the school by the headmaster, along with the other three newly qualified teachers – all of us could all be spotted a mile off, as the stares of the established members of staff focused intently on us, making an initial assessment as to whether we could handle what lay ahead. I had met the maths department, who seemed really nice, very supportive, experienced and full of advice and encouragement. The head of Year 8 had spent some time with me going through information regarding various members of my form group, most of which entered and left my head in seconds as, at this stage, they were just abstract names to me. In addition, I had substantial notes from their previous tutor, who had left the school to secure a head of department position. He was extremely experienced but I could tell that he had been challenged throughout the year by the group, my new form group, 8NS. As my teaching career has gone on, I have learnt to enjoy inset days, as they ease you into the school year and provide rare opportunities to talk to colleagues, both socially and professionally, without thinking about when the bell for the next lesson will ring.

However, on that day, the reality of what lay ahead was being brought closer and closer through conversations which just served to slowly build on my already present anxiety and self-doubt. The day was approaching but I kept avoiding its gaze for as long as I could. Whose idea was it to go on this ride, anyway?

Why on earth would you want to be a teacher?

I truly am in awe of those people who knew they wanted to be a teacher from an early age. They have never considered anything else as they travel purposefully through the education system to fulfil their

CHAPTER 1 **THE STARTER**

dream. That is not me. I had never even remotely entertained the idea of becoming a teacher – why would I? It lacks glamour, is respected by few, pays little in comparison to other professions I could have gone into (as a maths graduate), and seemed like really hard work for little reward. I have always had a knack for maths; it just makes sense to me and, even when I was in my teens, I was intrigued by the beauty in numbers, patterns and order. I especially enjoyed studying history too, but writing essays was something I had to work much harder at, and words did not flow for me so easily onto a page compared to equations.

I was halfway through the final year of my Mathematics and Statistics degree and had absolutely no clue what I wanted to do next. I had flirted with the idea of accounting or finance but just did not feel any inspiration or excitement about those careers. So, of course, I did what any young person with little direction or ideas would do – I did what my mates were doing! In addition, studying for a PGCE meant I could stay for another year at the same university, which had become all too comfortable. I was not ready for the real world quite yet. To say that I fell into teaching for an 'easy' fourth year is the sad truth. I am still in awe, but slightly suspicious, of those people who always knew they wanted to be a teacher – do such people really exist? Yes, I have met many such wonderful souls and we need to ensure that their dream is kept alive and not broken due to workload or behaviour management issues that can really take away all the positives of teaching.

Why write this book?

I feel hugely passionate about the teaching profession. I strongly believe that all children deserve to be taught by caring, understanding, patient and inspirational teachers. I truly believe that these are present in all schools and (more so) that there are thousands of potential teachers out there who just don't know it yet and like a younger me, have never considered it as a path. I remember completing my PGCE and realising that it did not prepare me well enough for being a 'real' teacher. I also recognise that this was partly due to my casual approach at the time, but nevertheless I was allowed to 'play' at teaching for the most part during my training year. I have since supported numerous trainees in programmes that expose them to the reality of the classroom but do not necessarily prepare them for the challenging and hectic life of a new teacher.

I do not wish to sound negative. Teaching is such an enjoyable and emotionally fulfilling job and, once established in a school, the long hours and feelings of stress do reduce, but it is also incredibly draining and hard work in the initial years. I believe that more can be done to bridge the gap between training and the first few years.

The Early Career Framework, introduced in 2021, attempts to give greater support to new teachers. The framework provides *'a funded entitlement to a structured 2-year package of high-quality professional development.'* The induction period for teachers has been extended from one year to two, meaning that slightly lighter timetables will be given to new teachers ('early career teachers') for a longer period, to help them take the step up without feeling overburdened or out of their depth. In-school support from subject mentors has been made more rigorous, with increased training (from external providers) for those staff being a requirement to ensure that the new teacher is guided and developed as effectively as possible. In addition, schools should continue to provide a lead induction tutor to oversee the support. The 2012 Teachers' Standards are maintained as the defined set of skills that all teachers should be able to demonstrate and therefore are judged against.

We need to protect those new to the profession and not drown them with bureaucracy. Evidence and justification of successfully meeting the Teachers' Standards can become solely a paper exercise that takes the judgement and trust out of mentors, heads of department and school leadership. Time will tell whether the framework can be an upgrade on the previous system, improving the quality of those new into the profession as well as reducing those leaving the profession early in their teaching careers, by ensuring that expectations are realistic. I am hopeful of the new system, but we – training providers, teaching schools and school leaders – must regularly question ourselves to ensure that support for trainees and early career teachers is meaningful, effective, focused and targeted. This will ensure that precious and limited time is not wasted as they try to navigate the workload mountain. We must not add unnecessary levels that make the peak even higher.

CHAPTER 1 **THE STARTER**

I appreciate that there are limitations on training programmes and we desperately need to increase the numbers entering the profession, but I groan inside when I see a government advert for teaching with smiley children, often in small classes, in inspiring and uplifting situations. This does happen sometimes, but highlights only a tiny proportion of what teaching is all about. It seems that sometimes we are duping people into teaching with exaggerated public relations and (not insignificant) bursaries, training them with an emphasis on collecting evidence, rather than experience, to then leave them to sink or swim in the deep waters of the life of a newly qualified or early career teacher. It should not be underestimated how different the first few years of being a 'real teacher' are when compared to the preparation and training that is given. Why do about a third of teachers leave the profession before completing their first five years? We must work harder and be more innovative with strategies for training and development, to support those who, unsurprisingly, find the job challenging.

Quite rightly, education is increasingly becoming influenced and impacted by research. As practitioners, we are encouraged to continually experiment with different types of questioning, assessment, technology and learning activities designed to engage students and build their deep understanding. We grow their character, resilience, motivation, confidence, aspiration and passion for learning. We narrow the gap. We support wellbeing and mental health. We build good habits in our students, strengthen skills in their comfort zone and enhance their thinking in new areas. We teach our subjects but, more importantly, guide and develop the young people in our care. All of this is incredibly important and demonstrates what a truly wonderful profession teaching is.

But the vital truth (which sometimes gets lost in advertising, training, policies and inspections) is that **if you cannot get your students to behave then you will achieve nothing** and you will become more and more negative about teaching as a result. It is heartbreaking to see someone, often someone who has always wanted to be a teacher, full of brilliant ideas and a righteous sense of purpose, fail to command a classroom and fail to reach their dream. Even worse, it then becomes taboo and they do their best to hide their struggles from colleagues who might be doing and experiencing the same things with the same classes or students.

CHAPTER 1 **THE STARTER**

It is interesting to note that only one of the eight sections in the 2012 Teachers' Standards, which we are judged on, in our training year and beyond, refers to behaviour:

7. Manage behaviour effectively to ensure a good and safe learning environment

- *have clear rules and routines for behaviour in classrooms, and take responsibility for promoting good and courteous behaviour both in classrooms and around the school, in accordance with the school's behaviour policy*

- *have high expectations of behaviour, and establish a framework for discipline with a range of strategies, using praise, sanctions and rewards consistently and fairly*

- *manage classes effectively, using approaches which are appropriate to pupils' needs in order to involve and motivate them*

- *maintain good relationships with pupils, exercise appropriate authority, and act decisively when necessary.*

(Source: https://assets.publishing.service.gov.uk/media/5a750668ed915d3c7d529cad/Teachers_standard_information.pdf)

I decided to write this book to place an emphasis in teaching on behaviour and wellbeing, at a time when the public perception seems that it is a given that students and classes will behave and, if they don't, it is either their fault or the fault of ineffective school leadership. I believe this is rarely the case, as the large majority of students want well-ordered lessons where they will learn something or at least experience a calm, controlled climate. Certainly, school leaders would not want to create an environment that does not establish positive behaviour for learning.

I have collected strategies, ideas and teaching habits that just might work for you in your classroom, in the same way that they have worked for me or my many wonderful colleagues over the years. They mostly require little preparation (although you may need time to tweak ideas so that they work for you). The ones that are effective for you will make the job – and your life – easier and more enjoyable. Making improvements in any area is often the result of applying and then sustaining small or simple changes to achieve those marginal gains that we keep hearing about. I hope that some ideas resonate enough for you to try them out with classes, and then that they work well enough for you to build them into part of your routines.

I have written this book for anyone interested in going into teaching, anyone training to be a teacher, newly and recently qualified teachers, experienced teachers moving to a new school and anyone who is just wanting some inspiration for their classroom. I hope that established teachers will recognise many ideas from their own practice but might also discover new approaches. It is fair to say that in this book there is an emphasis on secondary school teaching, due to my personal experience, but establishing effective routines for behaviour is a challenge that all teachers, and anyone else working with groups of children, need to overcome, whatever their environment.

Like anyone, my approaches into managing an effective classroom are shaped by my journey and experiences in education.

MY JOURNEY
Learning (or not) at school

Effective teachers hone their skills by utilising intuition and empathy. We need to understand how our students are feeling during our lessons. We need to be able to relate to the motivated, the positive, the triers, the passive, the barely coping, the distracted, the disinterested, the negative and the disruptive. This can be difficult, especially considering that often we, as teachers, have benefited from, and even enjoyed, our education. However, I am sure that, if we all search hard enough, we can unearth sufficient examples of poor teaching. We can remember what we considered boring and pointless lessons, or being present in disruptive classes, to help us appreciate the perceptions, mindsets and challenges of those we now teach.

CHAPTER 1 THE STARTER

It was only when I started teaching (teaching properly, not during my training year) that I forced myself to honestly reflect on the thousands of lessons that I had been a pupil in. My earliest clear memories of school go back to when I was 7 or 8 years old and I was in a junior school in Huddersfield. I remember the place fondly. It was a fairly small school, which meant that everyone, teachers and students alike, knew everyone else. The local area was very deprived and the negative reputation of local schools was an accepted part of life there. As someone who could pick up things well, I enjoyed being one of the top two or three in the class – this hid many of the teaching deficiencies present which failed to support less able students. I usually 'got' what the teachers were trying to deliver to us and, as a result, I got a relatively easy ride, including going early to playtime while others were punished for not being as 'good' (or, as I recall it being stated several times, not as 'clever'). I do not remember much variety or support for weaker students – what must the experience have been for those who were constantly lagging behind? I do recall that we judged our teachers on who controlled the class the best, some through fear, some through sarcasm and insults, and a few through the mutual respect that was clearly there for all to see. I also distinctly remember thinking that some teachers did not like teaching and/or spending time with children – though at the time this fact did not seem at all odd to me.

The natural progression was then to the partner secondary school. Some of my friends were moved to other schools (including some private schools) in order to avoid the perceived horrors and inadequacies that the rest of us would have to face. Several years later, while watching the 1969 Ken Loach film *Kes*, I was reminded of my high school as I drew so many parallels with the school scenes in the excellent adaptation of the book, *A Kestrel for a Knave*. I did enjoy my time there, despite it being what might be considered today as a dysfunctional, inadequate and failing school. I continued to benefit from being one of the more able students and, when it came to subjects that I was not so natural at (mostly practical lessons), I learnt to keep quiet and avoid any undue attention, with the teachers finding themselves occupied by several disruptive elements in my class. I do remember some engaging teachers whose lessons I enjoyed due to the relaxing but controlled classroom environment, with a clear focus on making sure everyone benefited from the teaching, whatever their level. However, my mind is always drawn back to two clear teaching

CHAPTER 1 **THE STARTER**

styles that still make me shudder to this day – those who ruled through fear, using the physical punishment that teachers were afforded at the time, and those who had no control whatsoever, watching helplessly as the class ran wild and the children largely dictated how the lessons would play out.

Fear and physical punishments were considered normal. I clearly remember lessons where 'naughty' children were asked to have a quiet word with a teacher outside or in a nearby office or empty classroom and, after a few minutes of hearing raised voices and mysterious banging or slamming, the child would return looking hurt (physically and emotionally). This was one 'effective' way to control a class that was probably accepted, allowed and even encouraged in most schools at the time. (Don't worry, those strategies did not make it into this book!) Interestingly, the best teachers at the school did not ever need to – or, I am sure, would never want to – resort to the cane or the threat of a chat in the 'room of doom', as they were able to win our hearts and minds through **simple, effective teaching.**

I am sure that we all remember being students in lessons where we actively engaged (or participated through limited choice) in actions designed to test the patience and sanity of the teacher, sending them crazy, making them angry or leaving the room upset. Why would anyone want to be a teacher subjected to that kind of psychological abuse? How bad must things be for you to choose that torture as your daily working life? Feeling sorry for the teacher is something that we all did but with no, or little, self-control. What else would you expect a group of young people to do in an environment where we were the dominant force? I am sure that some of my late-August teacher nightmares, which we will get to later, are recreations, in part, of those lessons.

After a few years in that school, my family moved to Crawley and I had to be the new boy in the class for the first time in my life – looking and sounding quite different to everyone else with my topknot and equally alien strong Yorkshire accent. Do not ever underestimate how difficult it is for a new student to join a school where friendships, relationships and accepted student hierarchies and groups are already established. Despite this, I was confident that my academic ability would ensure things would not be too bad. However, I had moved from a small struggling school to a much larger successful one, and I was brought

CHAPTER 1 **THE STARTER**

to the harsh reality of my new environment when I was only put in Set 3 for maths. Inside, I was broken, but it did serve a purpose as my (mostly) unhelpful inner arrogance, which had been built through being a top dog, was dented at its foundations. It was not a total disaster, though, as the school had a 15-form entry and grouped students into three levels, and I was tremendously relieved when I was put in the top tier. This was my first experience of the different dynamics that can come from ability setting.

Generally, I remember better teaching, less disruptive behaviour and more ordered classrooms than in my previous school. Was this as a result of the streaming, having students from more aspirational backgrounds or simply being a school with better exam results? However, I also remember lessons where the 'able' students would be more devious and subtle about how they expertly took a teacher apart. I have learnt that, unless students 'buy in' to the teacher and teaching style, chaos and misbehaviour will follow, regardless of the school context and whatever the ability of the students. In this school, effective teachers brought their subject to life more than I had experienced before, and they created an open but controlled learning environment. My love for history developed through fantastically engaging and knowledgeable teachers who made the subject relevant. More surprisingly for me, my appreciation for the importance of English and literacy developed as a result of a fantastic English teacher's slightly eccentric and almost hypnotic teaching style, which was full of anecdotes, opinions and a loose structure. This formed my total fascination with the story and language of Shakespeare's *Richard III*. In contrast, what did I do in those lessons where I did not have the passion or enjoyment? I kept quiet, did little and, because I was not causing a problem, I managed to get away with it lesson after lesson, week after week and year after year. Yes, I did get my comeuppance when I was forced to choose a GCSE in Craft, Design and Technology (or CDT as we called it then) with no basic skills for, interest in, or understanding of, the subject.

Reflecting on my years in school, I had some questions that I needed to find answers to if I was going to make it – or just survive – in teaching:

1. How did some teachers make it look so easy? They didn't have to do anything to manage behaviour; it just happened naturally.

CHAPTER 1 THE STARTER

2. What were the 'bad' teachers doing wrong? Their intentions were honest, they had clearly planned lessons and they knew what they were talking about, but it seemed like the class would not let them do their job.

3. How important for behaviour was the school's environment, reputation and success? My first teaching job was in a school which at the time was considered challenging and towards the bottom of league tables. Was I already doomed to failure?

Teaching looks so easy

I vividly remember the first time I was thrust into a classroom situation as a student teacher, a few months into my PGCE year. We had spent the first part of the course in university lecture theatres, trying to absorb key aspects of the psychology of learning and teaching. At the time, I convinced myself that this information was irrelevant to what I needed to know about the 'real' classroom. However, I engaged passively, as I was still only playing at being a teacher and, the longer I was kept from the true job, I could keep on pretending that this year would be just like my previous three years at the University of East Anglia.

My first teaching practice placement was in a lovely rural high school in Norfolk, academically not the best but it had real warmth and a true sense of purpose to support the needs of its young people. I spent two or three weeks just observing lessons delivered by experienced teachers, speaking to a variety of established staff and meeting with carefully selected students. From this I gauged that **teaching was easy**. The classes were generally well behaved and the teachers did not seem to need to do anything to achieve this. When listening was required, the teacher would calmly give the command and, within 15 seconds or so, there was quiet. Yes, there were episodes of poor behaviour, either from an individual or small groups within a class, but the teacher was still able to deal with what was going on and retain control. This was not the case in a few lessons and with a minority of teachers, but it was with the seven or eight staff that I was placed with. Being a bit wet behind the ears, I assumed that this was the norm across the school. My conclusion, therefore, was that teaching

CHAPTER 1 **THE STARTER**

was easy and, as long as I knew my subject and planned well enough, then there would be no huge problems during my training year and certainly beyond.

Teachers who make it look easy don't shout, they hardly ever raise their voice, they know their students extremely well, have positive relationships, are respected, and have an uncanny knack for spotting disruption at the early stages and then deliberately changing the direction of the lesson to re-establish focus and control. Most of all, they enjoy being in the classroom. Yes, they also know their subject, plan well, vary student activities, use different types of questioning, assess effectively, scaffold learning and model all the other skills we are introduced to during training. I would say it took me at least two years of being a proper teacher to get anywhere near to all of this. Is that just the norm for everyone? If so, is this reality clearly shared with trainees from the outset? It might reduce the numbers of teachers leaving so early in their career because of a perception that they are failing, that they are unable to cut it in the classroom, that they will never be able to conquer the workload mountain or be able to see the incredible job that they will do in the years ahead. More so, how does this impact their self-confidence? It gets easier for almost all of us, but it does take time and it does require trying many varied strategies to see what works, as well as accepting that 'simple wins' might work on most occasions, but could fail miserably at other times for no obvious reason.

The ineffective teachers

So, what about the 'bad' teachers? I use the term 'bad' not because any teacher should be labelled in that way but it is a term that students will use when doing their own analysis of the competencies of the adult in front of them. I confess that I would put myself in this category when reflecting on my first few years – maybe, harshly, many of us would. During my first year, I think I was happy with two of my seven classes: Year 7 and a lower sixth form (Year 12) group. There were groups I think I did an OK job with some of the time, groups where the balance of power was far more even, and then a Year 10 lower set group which filled me with dread. It occupied my thoughts for a large part of the week, making me doubt my skills and abilities as well as really testing

CHAPTER 1 **THE STARTER**

my patience and sanity. Why do those devious people who design school timetables always seem to place me with such groups on a Friday afternoon? Fairly regular thoughts at the end of the week, in the pub with my colleagues, were: 'Did I really want to be a teacher?' and 'What was so bad that had put me off going into accountancy and finance?' In my opinion, most 'bad' teaching, or ineffective strategies, stems from a lack of control. From the very start to the welcome end of a lesson, which cannot come soon enough, too many students are not listening, not concentrating, not working and not respecting instructions or authority. I am not referring to the individual students that most teachers in a school would struggle with, but to a significant minority in the group. The one thing that those students are doing, though, is clearly being in control of the classroom.

Teaching is not for everyone. I am sure that we have all had those conversations with friends, family or strangers we have just been introduced to as 'a teacher'. They say: 'I don't know how you do it', 'They couldn't pay me enough to teach other people's kids, I struggle with my own', 'I have so much respect for you', 'I hated being at school', 'I'd end up hitting one of them' or simply 'Why? You must be crazy?'. (I won't mention the comments about all the holidays!) These are conversations which we smile through but don't dent our resolve. Only a select few are lucky enough to end up as teachers, whether it is part of a long-term plan or whether it is a result of an unpredictable fate. No teacher enters the profession content to be in the 'bad' category, not really caring about the job they are doing and being happy to just to go through the motions in order to pay the bills. Teaching isn't like that – it truly becomes a part of you that you cannot switch on at 8:30am and pause at 4pm. Teachers who are struggling with behaviour need to accept it, seek advice, try to persist with new strategies, remain positive, know that things will improve over time and, importantly, remind themselves of why they went into the profession and the difference they can – and will – make. These teachers (in fact all of us) need to be supported by the school leadership as well as by our departmental colleagues. It certainly is not easy. Teaching is relentless, classes can be unforgiving, workload is constant and the classroom can be a lonely place. No teacher is simply 'bad' or their strategies doomed to failure. Every school has great teachers to learn from. With focused effort and targeted support, things do get easier and, most importantly, remember that the large majority of students want to learn in a calm and purposeful environment. The beautiful, daunting, yet fully achievable, challenge is to win them over.

Battlelines, dreams and the phoney war

Power lies in numbers. The phoney war in the classroom has 30 young people on one side: a usually complex and gloriously unpredictable group armed with youthful exuberance but also a thirst for trust, respect and care. On the other side is the one, lonely teacher on a mission to establish order, carrying a range of weapons which largely act as threats but sometimes shoot blanks, misfire or explode in their own hands, creating a smoke cloud of embarrassment. We often play this battle out in our heads in our first few years of teaching and, just when we think we have perfected our skills, a new army catches us off guard and then we have to retreat, regroup, redesign our weaponry and rethink our strategy.

This is the beautiful challenge of teaching. This is the reason I have vivid dreams (usually in late August) that start with me standing in front of a peaceful classroom and then, slowly, I realise that my control is waning and all my tried-and-tested methods to regain the balance are doing nothing to stop the relentless march towards chaos. Raising my voice, introducing threats of detentions, getting angry, being as scary as I can ... nothing works. '*I have been teaching without major issues for years, this class is not a problem, this should not be happening. Why is this happening to me? What am I going to do next?*' Well, I wake up, take a deep breath, see that it is 2am and try to go back to sleep, acutely aware of the smile on my face as I mutter to myself, 'Wow, it has been a while since I have had one of those dreams!'. I used to think that I was the only person who had dreams like this and that it must have been linked to some hidden experience in my past that I did not want to uncover. However, in talking about it to many other teachers, it seems most of us share this unconscious self-doubt which catches us unaware in the middle of the night on one of the last few days of a break.

There is also a battle of the minds. One of the most debilitating attacks from the students comes in the form of the well-known **honeymoon period**. As new teachers to a class, we are tricked into thinking

CHAPTER 1 **THE STARTER**

the path is going to be smooth when our first few lessons are the things that pleasant dreams are made of: the whole class quietens immediately, students are attentive throughout as they follow your instructions to the letter, and at the end you are thanked for the lesson. The only thing missing is the apple placed on the teachers desk by one of these angels. The conforming clones are slowly replaced by real children over the first few weeks and, before you know it, you are really on the back foot because of their well-worked strategy. You may have heard the advice 'Don't smile until Easter' to help new teachers establish themselves as someone not to be messed with (or not to be tested) – that's not as easy as it sounds with this clever ruse at play. You can, of course, forgive your gullibility the first few times but, as you grow in experience, you can turn this attack back on the unsuspecting student group, continuing the honeymoon for much longer by using our go-to strategies. Once it is over, you are the confident classroom chief ruling your domain as you wish (well, mostly). However, just when you thought teaching was becoming predictable, you experience a class or a school where relationships don't start with honeymoons – then you know you are in trouble! This was a real shock to me when I first moved schools and was given the rudest of awakenings with a Year 10 class banging their desks and chanting as soon as I entered the room, not allowing my perfected first lesson introduction – 'My name is Mr Singh and …' – to even have a chance. How did I deal with this situation? Poorly, to say the least, but you'll read about that later, as I balance simple tips and advice with some key learning resulting from my teaching fails.

The factory

During my 25 years of teaching, I have had the pleasure of working with many excellent trainees and new teachers from a wide range of backgrounds and experiences, all ready to throw themselves into the hectic life of a teacher. But how do they balance that with their personal life, both in terms of their time and their mental energy? This is something which must be considered from the offset. It can be easier for those without a family, not having to work late after completing their evening shift in their most important role as mum or dad, but it can also be helpful to have someone outside of the school environment to keep things in perspective and provide emotional support.

CHAPTER 1 THE STARTER

I am finding that more and more trainees are career changers rather than coming straight from university, as I did. In my training cohort, most of the student teachers were in their early to mid-20s, and had fairly recent experience of being in the classroom as a student. I used to think this was important and gave us the edge over older trainees, but increasingly I am convinced of the benefits of being able to draw on a range of experiences, not just those in education. The ability to be reflective and then proactive is the most important thing. It is too easy to link energy and creativity with youthfulness and then associate wisdom and patience with experience. Challenges that trainees have to overcome are individual, whatever their situation. The important thing is to have a rooted desire to work with young people.

Trainees offer so much to schools – and I don't mean as people to take teachers' lessons and do their marking. They bring with them innocence, ideas and a desire for innovation. Experienced teachers must not forget that our teaching may have become routine and monotonous as we convince ourselves of the existence of a closed set of teaching strategies that we know 'work'. Trainees can question the norm – they want to establish for themselves what will be effective with classes and what will not. They should be encouraged to take risks in the protected environment they benefit from. However, remember that the life of a trainee and a new teacher is not easy.

I heard a wonderful description of the reason why things are so hard in the first few years, from a new teacher who had previous experience of working in the 'real world' – they called it **building and running your factory**. Experienced teachers have put strategies in motion to help them manage their role, having established themselves and having taught numerous lessons, often on the same topics, year on year. For them, the main task is the day-to-day running of their factory, which in itself is no mean feat. However, for new teachers, who have to build their factory from the foundations while concurrently running it, teaching is mentally and physically exhausting, relentless and leads to bouts of intense self-doubt. What more can we do to help?

I believe that we will better fulfil our responsibilities if we can shift the focus during the training period away from a paper exercise where we struggle to collect enough evidence to demonstrate that a trainee has met each of the Teachers' Standards. We need to move towards a training programme that has managing workload and establishing the right classroom environment at its core. We need to ensure that trainees are supported more effectively to manage the transition from being a 'student teacher' delivering a few lessons a day to a full-time professional who is expected to cope with a full day in the classroom. If we can do this then I firmly believe that fewer teachers will leave the profession in their early years and, most importantly, the learning and development of our young people will improve significantly.

The Early Career Framework is an attempt to correct this. I do not wish to criticise the range of the list and the Teachers' Standards, as I think they provide a clear guide for effective teaching, but, for trainees and newly qualified teachers trying to establish themselves, the balance needs to be different. In simple terms, if you take three hours to plan an hour's lesson and if you cannot get a class to behave, then you will achieve very little, however good you are at planning, assessment, questioning, being organised, using data and knowing your subject. If we don't make teaching easier, we will continue to experience significant teacher shortages, whatever teachers get paid. When I say 'easier', I am not talking about working less or cutting corners, because teaching is hard work no matter your experience, subject, role and type of school. I am talking more about the emotional strain where we can struggle to find confidence, belief and positivity. If teaching really was easy and we put our feet up for three months of the year when we have 'holidays', then schools would not face the regular recruitment pressures that are a constant headache for many school leaders.

Key principles

Great teaching, according to a 2014 Sutton Trust study, has six key components: subject knowledge, quality of instruction, classroom climate, classroom management, teacher beliefs and professional behaviours. Why do some teachers make it look so easy? Surely it is not as simple as the longer you teach, the better you get at it. I have worked with experienced and committed teachers who face the same classroom battles year on year, unable to move forward, as well as new teachers who seem to be naturals and can have even challenging classes eating out of their hand without using any obvious magic or mind tricks. This was as evident to me when I was a student at school as it is now.

When it comes to behaviour management, effective teaching is built around some obvious, but easy to forget or ignore, key principles:

Relationships

Winning hearts opens the door to minds. Young people need to know that you are invested in them, you enjoy getting to know them and you enjoy teaching them, even when they can be difficult. 'Why do you want to be a teacher?' is a common interview question. It allows you to give an insight into why you enjoy working with and developing young people, rather than just talking about wanting to deliver your subject to a group of robots who will follow their programming instructions to the letter without ever questioning them, or seeking to understand the rationale.

Fairness

Part of establishing a positive climate in your classroom involves dealing with disruptive and challenging behaviours through either verbal or school sanctions. This is a part of the job which is accepted by teachers and students alike: young people make mistakes, as we all do. Classrooms need to be environments where respect and learning can flourish. The role of the teacher is to ensure that there is a clear sense of purpose. This requires an easily understood and accepted set of rules which need to be adhered to. With this in mind, the way in which we actually deal with situations adds to the message about how we care about the young people we teach – all the young people, not just the 'good' ones who always follow the rules.

Consistency

Alongside being fair, we are judged on our consistency. Teaching can throw out the unexpected, where the same classes can behave differently for no apparent reason, yet **we** need to try to be consistent in our approach. For many young people, schools provide much-needed security and care, with a big part of this being not having to cope with adults who can present themselves as very 'up and down'. We are certainly allowed to have bad days and to overreact, but part of us being human also enables us to apologise when this has happened and acknowledge our mistakes. Moreover, if you need reassurance, teaching any group, however challenging, does get easier once they get to know you through your consistency and clarity. We are not perfect, but being too inconsistent in our manner will often initiate a game where students enjoy working out if it is a good day or a bad one where they can possibly enjoy an emotional firework display at our expense.

Patience

Teaching requires an incredible amount of patience. We rely on the many students in our class to make a success of a lesson and therefore they have a big say in our positivity and wellbeing. In the heat of the moment, it is easy to take things personally, as we feel pressure when we know that a carefully planned lesson is not working out as we had envisaged. It requires patience when instructions, or even polite requests, are not being followed quickly enough. We are again judged by students on how we react. However, too much patience can indicate a lack of interest or control on your part, so it is important to get that balance right. I never said it was easy!

Challenge

Effective teaching is not just about being a nice, balanced person who is fair and has oodles of patience. We do need to actually teach these young people. Your expectations of them, in terms of both their behaviour and learning ability, is important in moving towards a focused and purposeful classroom environment. Making things too easy in order to support lower performing students leaves others bored, yet catering for the top end of the class will alienate others – both of these approaches are a recipe for disaster. Being aware of your students' needs and providing suitable challenge to all does sound difficult, but only if lesson aims are too specific in what you are trying to achieve.

The ugly pandemic and the wonderful classroom

Teachers live and breathe for the buzz of being in the classroom, despite the challenges and unexpected twists and turns that can

CHAPTER 1 THE STARTER

reside there. It is this staple diet each day that feeds our professional hunger and, as a senior leader with reduced teaching, the moments in the classroom often re-energise me on days where long periods of time are spent meeting with other professionals, writing policies or thinking strategically. In March 2020, all that changed due to the Covid pandemic. Those not working in schools will find it difficult to fully appreciate the impact this had on the working life and mental health of teachers, in addition to what young people had to cope with. The classroom was now virtual. Teaching and assessment had to be massively redesigned, and interactions with our students were mostly at a superficial level via email or behind a blank screen due to faulty cameras or (more likely) young people not wanting to show their face online due to emotional challenges linked to self-esteem. Personally, I have never looked forward to meetings with other staff so much as during this period, even if they were over a screen.

It seemed that everything teachers had learnt over the years, and all the classroom skills that they had developed, were now temporarily redundant. I have huge amounts of sympathy, equally for experienced teachers nearing the end of their careers, who lacked confidence in online learning platforms, for teachers with young children and their own parental responsibilities, for newly qualified teachers or trainees in the early stages of honing their craft – and of course everyone in between. This undoubtedly has been the biggest challenge for teachers in generations and the impact on the teaching profession will be felt for years to come.

For me, a positive mindset was my biggest ally during those dark days, getting me through the challenges of online teaching that none of us had entered the profession to do. The reopening of schools and return to the wonderful classroom was truly emotional for me and, despite face coverings, spaced out desks, having to stay at the front without circulating, and teaching some students at school at the same time as supporting the learning of others in the same group at home, I was instantly reminded of the pleasure to be found in all corners of the classroom. Teachers are having to remind themselves of how to manage a 'normal classroom' again.

Yes, the pandemic now sits in a part of history that we will not want to revisit until the scars have healed and it has become a distant memory,

CHAPTER 1 **THE STARTER**

but there are some valuable lessons to be learnt by looking at the impact on teachers and teaching. Teaching is not a fixed profession, where we blindly follow an agreed set of rules and guidelines. Education is ever changing and the best schools appreciate the need to be flexible in their approach, to be open to learning from how others meet the needs of their students and to accept that what works today might need to be adapted to cope with the unknown future. The best teachers will thrive within this mindset.

Sharing good practice

I have openly and honestly written this book for anyone involved in teaching or considering it as a potential career path. We all need inspiration, reminders and questions which force us to reflect on our own journey and motivations – even more so after the impact of lockdown and online learning. As we journey on to my list of (hopefully) useful strategies and embarrassing mistakes, it is important to think carefully about what resonates with you, what fits into your style, your context, your needs, your strengths and weaknesses.

Reflecting on my own skills, thinking about the excellent colleagues I have worked with and speaking to professionals from other schools has led me to create this (not exhaustive) list. When you find things that you want to try, appreciate the need to persevere and adapt before you decide they are not working. Experienced teachers will have taught thousands of lessons and still not truly perfect a strategy, due to the evolution of the student army and the shifting focus in education.

Finally, remember the immense pleasure and excitement which teaching brings. There is nothing wrong with enjoying yourself in the classroom – why should students have all the fun?

Enjoy!

CHAPTER 2 **BEST OF THE BEST**

Within a few months of being in the classroom, we start firming up the list of 'things' which have worked for us. These are not the same for everyone, as we differ in our approaches, our strengths, our habits, our character, our interests, the way in which we want to deliver our subject, the ideas we feel most comfortable with, and the context of our classes and school. We don't always know why certain strategies are effective but, as we start teaching, we are on high alert to divide what we do into what seems to work and what does not.

However, we must accept that sometimes approaches we might try take time to perfect and shape into key parts of our armoury. We must not give up on strategies too quickly as there are always elements of unpredictability, lack of logic and human irrationality beating away in the heart of the classroom which could render even the most inspirational of ideas temporarily useless. As we become more experienced, those mischievous elements usually fall under our control as we develop a third intuitive eye, always ready to deploy Plan B, C, D, E …

Despite this key challenge within teaching, most of us will find largely failsafe teaching strategies which form our go-to classroom habits, influencing our facial expressions, body language, tone of voice and commonly used phrases and words. Here are mine.

CHAPTER 2 **BEST OF THE BEST**

1 Thank you, it has been a pleasure

I want you to imagine that you are walking into a training session with teachers from a range of other schools, being delivered by the 'expert' at some picturesque venue far away from your usual day-to-day existence. How quickly do you make up your mind about how effective and useful the next few hours are going to be for you? Is it as soon as you go into the venue and see the quality of the refreshments or the range of sweets on the table? Is it when you get your first glance at the presenter – their age, their clothes, their confidence or facial expression? Maybe it is nothing to do with the presenter, but is linked to whether you spot a fellow delegate who you recognise? Or does it take longer for you to decide? Will you give it the first 15 minutes before predicting how much you will learn?

The question I would ask, while you are capturing your mood in this scenario, is **how important is it to you that the presenter seems to be enjoying delivering their training**, as opposed to it coming across as a chore?

In front of a challenging group of students, it is hard to hide your anxiety, lack of confidence, annoyance or even dread. In fact, it is natural to act disappointed if you are indeed disappointed, and it seems false to smile in a fit of overwhelming positivity when things are not going as planned.

How you appear in front of your students is important. I cannot stress this enough.

A great way of developing a positive frame of mind is to ensure that you deliver simple but effective and uplifting messages throughout your lesson. *'Good morning, it is great to see you all'*, *'I'm really looking forward to our lesson together'*, *'Thank you'*, *'Really well done for today's lesson. I enjoyed it and felt we achieved so much'*. OK, so some of you might be contemplating how well you will be able to convincingly and genuinely deliver those lines to classes where the battle just to get them quiet has not yet been won. Positive feedback can be disarming and benefit both your and your students' wellbeing, especially if it is not the norm for you to say, or for them to hear. It can also make you more resilient in the mental combat of the classroom.

Do you really want to come across as someone who does not enjoy teaching the group and as someone who would rather criticise than praise?

2 Let the good kids win

Our schools and classrooms function on a set of rules and expectations that often form the background of the difficulties that teachers will face, especially in the first few years. It is easy, as a teacher, to become obsessive about instances when students fail to meet the most basic of requirements. As a result, much of our time is spent reminding and reprimanding the perpetrators while unfortunately ignoring the victims. They are victims because their learning is being disrupted but more so because their engagement and compliance is going unnoticed and is being taken for granted.

An interesting thought, which can challenge schools and teachers (because, if true, it would throw into confusion the idea of establishing order via rules) is that the students whom you are regularly telling off continue to behave the same lesson after lesson and therefore the arsenal of punishments at your disposal is practically useless. Maybe something else is going on here. Students who thrive on, and are hungry for, attention – both from you and their peers – can quickly learn that the simplest way to achieve their desired outcome is to misbehave or to keep jumping over the line you have drawn in the sand. This can make you more determined to up the ante and face off one-on-one in a battle where you think you have the upper hand but, unfortunately, most of the time you will lose. I personally have never been a fan of the strategy that some teachers deploy, and some schools recommend – writing students' names 'on the board' when anyone steps out of line – three strikes and you're out. This not only further emphasises the negatives in your classroom but also dishes out much sought-after attention to those who display poor behaviour, telling the rest of the class that it is this small group of students who will dictate the direction of the lesson. We will return to this idea when I share my teacher fails.

Remember the victims, the 'good kids'? There are many examples of educational research which suggest that the optimal ratio for positive to negative feedback from a teacher is about 6:1. I would suggest that this is a minimum, as there should not be a ceiling on positive reinforcement, if it is deserved. So, rather than telling off students for not following a rule or direct instruction, shift your focus to the 'good kids' who you can praise, praise and praise some more for doing what you have asked, in the face of tempting distractions.

Simple changes to your language can move the emphasis on who is getting your attention, for example *'Really well done to those of you who have settled'* rather than *'I'm still waiting for some of you to be quiet and listen. Harry, Rachel … will you please stop talking?'*.

Build regular systems of reward for those students, including feeding back to parents, and you will slowly see more students wanting to be a part of the group who has your attention. Not all of them, of course – you will still have the few who will challenge and seek to disrupt. If teaching was that easy then it would not be so fulfilling, would it?

3 Really make them think at the start of the lesson

What happens in the first few minutes will often set the tone and thus dictate the success of a lesson. If we are unable to establish calm and purpose, it is likely that we will lose the battle before it has really begun. Yet, if you can demonstrate that this is 'our' classroom, centred around our rules and expectations that students will adhere to, then you have firm foundations from which you can build.

However, do not think that you need to start each lesson with a lecture on what behaviour you expect from the students. You would have done this the first few times you saw the class and if you then need to repeat your ground rules at length then you are sending the message that they have the upper hand. A quick, short *'A reminder that I expect X'*, as part of your dialogue, is more effective. Calm and purpose can be effectively established through engaging their brains, reminding them unconsciously that your classroom is a place where enjoyable learning takes place.

We all know the numerous benefits to behaviour and learning of an effective starter activity, but vary your approach so that it does not become too predictable or monotonous. Students can enter classrooms with a mischievous spirit paired with a lack of focus and your job is to redirect their energy quickly. Design short 'do now' tasks that draw their interest as soon as they enter your classroom. Activities that require them to trawl their brains for information that they partially remember, make judgements and predictions, draw on their competitive natures or simply build confidence and positivity remind them that they enjoy the success that comes from being taught by you.

The best tasks that I have seen (and used) include problem solving to set up new learning, the use of anagrams to remind about key vocabulary, including in language lessons, open questions guiding students towards different viewpoints, and short retrieval quizzes to test previous knowledge. Silent reading can certainly deliver the calm that you desire and *directed* reading can set the scene for new learning with great effect.

4 Stock balls and doosras

In addition to teaching, one of my passions is cricket – both watching and, when I have the time, playing it. I realised quickly that I would not have the height or speed to provide any real menace as a fast bowler, so as a young teen I was drawn towards the art and mystery of spin bowling. Watching the likes of Shane Warne, Anil Kumble or Muttiah Muralitharan take just a few paces and, with a flick of their wrists or a twist of their fingers, bowl a magical delivery that left the batsman perplexed and often out-thought, enticed me into this art of confusion. It's due to the possible unpredictability. Stock balls are the bowler's most frequent type of delivery and so the one that the batsman gets used to, but out of nowhere comes the doosra (meaning 'the other one') that spins off in a different direction, often to great effect.

The battle in the classroom is fought as much in the mind as anywhere else.

Young people bring into the classroom an element of unpredictability but we, as teachers, aim to establish control by countering with consistency, through common practices and learning activities that are tried and tested and almost always achieve success. However, there is a danger that our lessons always follow the same pattern so, over time, they become dull or predictable and students find ways to add their own entertainment and fun at our expense. Remember the excitement of the unknown 'the first time'? Trying a different type of lesson does take nerve, but you need to appreciate that varying activities should not result in a loss of control. It often strengthens your longer-term position.

However, using the doosra too often reduces the effect, so again it is about getting the balance right. If your stock lessons are centred around PowerPoints, textbooks, think-pair-share discussions or a standard three-part structure (see page 43), then experiment on the odd occasion – and initially with the safest class at the safest time – with outdoor lessons, learning through discovery, student-led and designed activities, or entirely open-ended tasks. Even something as simple as teaching from the back of the classroom can be an effective doosra.

It is easy to develop habits based on what we think works without realising the loss of innovation that this brings. Consider the anticipation and excitement of developing into that creative teacher that brought you into the profession.

5 Replace the word 'work' with 'learning'

We know that language and words have great power, often through their directness and simplicity. They can effortlessly inspire, motivate and build confidence but in equal measure can easily have the opposite effect. We carefully consider what we should say when we first see a new class, rehearsing those crucial lines in our head over and over, but then relegate the importance of our words as time goes on. This is not a criticism, just an observation, as we have so much else that consumes our thinking.

My moment of inspiration here came from a training course I attended led by Guy Claxton, the great advocate of 'Learning Power', where he challenged us to replace the word 'work' with 'learning' when talking to students. I was dubious and (like most of you) had heard of this gimmicky trick before, yet something about his delivery convinced me to try it for a period of time, possibly just to prove him wrong.

The impact was immediate, unexpected and brilliant, more than justifying the £250 from my school's continuing professional development (CPD) budget. (I did gain much more from the course too by the way; otherwise it could have been reduced from a whole day to two minutes.) Talking to students about learning, rather than work, shifts the mindset of both them and you. Consider the difference in your head when hearing 'challenging learning' as opposed to 'difficult work'. Work is a cold, tedious, repetitive and uninspiring task that we have to do, yet learning can bring with it thoughts of adventure and exploration. This is not a type of hypnotism that turns everyone in front of you into learning lemmings and will solve all your problems in the classroom, but is the simplest of wins that does work (sorry, I should not be using that word, should I? But you know what I mean). However, it does require persistence on your part, as it is easy to fall back into the habit of talking about work, work, work.

6 Find out about the best teachers in your school and ask yourself why

I asked earlier why some teachers make the job look so easy. There is usually a multifaceted answer to this question which takes into account areas such as experience, subject and personality, as well as school context. Although the skeleton of a great teacher does not change, different schools bring with them different challenges. Having moved schools three times in my career, I appreciate the need to adjust to your new surroundings and accept that you may need to find out all over again what strategies could be effective as you build a new set of stock techniques and lessons.

Every school will have excellent practitioners who won't be advertised on an 'employee of the month' board in the staffroom but it will not be too difficult to track them down by speaking to those who support you when you join. Ensure that you go beyond the comfort of your department team, as you should learn from your close colleagues anyway. These leading lights around the school will be humble about their skills and may be unaware of the secrets behind their success, convincing themselves that '*I don't do anything special, I just teach*'. Your task is to dig deeper and investigate the roots that make the tree so strong, looking beneath the soil. Find out as much as you can about these teachers – I am not talking about stalking them, of course! Observe their interactions with students, not just in the classroom but around the school. Speak to students about what they enjoy in those lessons. Every teacher is different and you cannot exactly replicate the approach of someone else, but you can make small changes as a result of being influenced by colleagues who make being excellent look so effortless.

7 Accept that it will take time (and focus on the positives)

Being a great teacher does not come without first walking the long road in the rain. Making it look 'easy' certainly does take time and, unfortunately, there is no quick fix. The first few years will undoubtedly be the most challenging – remember the factory that we are building (see page 22)? Writing about how it will take time to become the teacher you want to be is no stroke of genius on my part, but hopefully it gets us to reflect on the emotional drain of having high expectations and unselfish intentions from the outset, while accepting that we cannot yet clearly see the beautiful scenery, as it is too far away. I remember feeling this pain for the first few years of teaching and then again in the first few months of each new school.

How do we protect ourselves from this potentially cruel blow to our confidence? My simple advice is twofold. Firstly, surround yourself with positive and honest colleagues and friends who will give constructive advice and encourage you by talking about the progress you have made. Secondly, take ownership of the situation by breaking down your (two-year) improvement plan into smaller, manageable parts, such as taking less time to plan, having quiet parts of lessons or building greater student engagement. Then assess yourself against these measures compared to your starting point.

This can apply to new teachers as well as those looking to push forward in their practice. The learning process is never ending and often the greatest improvements are made at the start of a journey. We often lose sight of this as our attention faces forward, towards a destination that we sometimes convince ourselves is not getting any closer. Remember that once you had never been the 'real' teacher, and had little confidence when speaking to students, let alone managing planning lessons, assessing learning and controlling the classroom. Do not focus on the negatives and failures without paying at least as much attention to the positives and successes.

8 Hands-down questioning

When I first started to seriously consider going into teaching, thoughts of being in front of a class largely filled me with trepidation. However, nestled beside the fear of not being able to manage behaviour were the warm, glowing moments that I could imagine of inspiring young people through creative and enjoyable activities. Those magic moments when you ask a class a question and the eager hands shoot up, stretching out all the way to the tips of the fingers in an effort to catch your attention. The excitement your students feel, in anticipation of being the lucky ones answering your question, giving you the correct answer and receiving your affirmation and praise. I saw such a scene on a recent advert encouraging more people to take the leap and enter the teaching profession.

Now pause for a moment, take a step back and consider a panoramic view of the whole classroom.

As a child, I remember lessons where I was largely passive, due to a lack of either interest or confidence. The same two or three students would answer questions correctly, meaning that the lesson could move on exactly as the teacher wanted and I could look at the scenery from the passenger seat. Occasionally, the teacher would show signs of mild frustration with a comment like *'You two are doing all the hard work here. I want someone else to answer this question'* and then the rest of us would go into mild panic and switch on our thinking. However, after a few answers lacking the required precision and perfection, the teacher would realise why asking the chosen few helped everyone get through the lesson unscathed.

Questioning is such an important part of great lessons and we have to explore its purpose. Is it simply to hear correct answers and move on, or to gauge the understanding of all students (rather than a few) and then review if needed, or to encourage engagement, participation and build confidence? The truth is it can be a mix of all those things.

CHAPTER 2 BEST OF THE BEST

However, it should not be a predictable part of the lesson that splits the class into those who know and are therefore involved, and those who don't and are therefore inactive.

When I observe lessons, I reflect on this and ask the teacher whether any student is allowed to be passive during questioning. Hands-down questioning – more fashionably referred to as 'cold calling' – helps to create a learning environment where everyone is involved. Confidence is built through courage. Mistakes are treated with equal importance as correct answers and help to move understanding forward. The teacher is firmly in control of proceedings, rather than it being a random and unpredictable part of the lesson. Excellent teachers will know their students and recognise those who may be apprehensive about being put on the spot, so will choose questions carefully, with elements of support where needed. A key element of effective questioning must be giving time for students to think. 'Cold calling' should not involve immediate on-the-spot feedback without a chance to consider what is being asked. I do understand that sometimes we want questioning to be quick, such as when reviewing previous learning and when defining clear facts or statements. However, by making hands-down questioning your usual approach, and by learning the skill of responding to a range of answers that may take learning in different directions, you will better serve all students. You may unearth magic that cannot be seen so easily in a 20-second recruitment advert. Try it, stick at it and you will notice the difference.

To enhance this teacher win, consider what you are trying to achieve and therefore how the order of your words can have the impact that you desire. You want all the students in your class to use their brains and think deeply, in the event that they may be the 'lucky' one who is chosen. Which of the following will be most effective?

- 'David, how does this character show empathy?'

- 'How does this character show empathy, David?'

- 'How does this character show empathy?... Erm' (pause for 30 seconds) 'David.'

- 'I want you all to think about how this character shows empathy for one minute and then I will get some feedback from two or three of you.'

Just because you employ a recognised and accepted classroom strategy, it does not mean that it will produce the desired outcome without a bit of tinkering. Any strategy can be done badly or simply at a surface level – I can definitely testify to that.

9 Stand up, sit down

This next simple win baffles the mind and pushes us to consider why students follow some instructions so promptly, and not others.

The irritation at the start of a lesson when you are trying to get your class to be quiet can be very wearing and, more importantly, set a negative tone as you repeat the need to settle and be ready for the lesson to start. Even the trick of getting students to line up in silence outside before you bring them in can backfire as you go through the battle twice, before and then, irritatingly, again after they have entered the classroom. Through experimentation and after several requests for a class to be quiet, I decided to tell them to stand up – incredibly, they all did within seconds even though only a few heard my instruction. One student stood up and then others decided they should do the same and quickly the whole class was standing up without fully knowing why but, even more surprisingly, they became deadly silent. When I tried this with a more stubborn group, they stood up but some were still talking so I asked them to sit down and, once they had become comfortable in their seats, I asked them to stand up again. They quietened down gradually and then I gave instructions and started the lesson before asking them to be seated.

When there is noise in the classroom and you demand quiet, some students will not hear you and others will wait until they think you are really being serious before following your instructions. When you ask them to stand up, it is likely that most will do this after just one request. Like any simple win, if it is used too often it will become less effective or turn into a game, so consider the 'when and how' carefully. However, this can act as a key reminder to all about who is in control of proceedings in your classroom.

CHAPTER 2 **BEST OF THE BEST**

10 **Be a great form tutor**

During my time in teaching, I have always thoroughly enjoyed being a form tutor. In fact, the daily interaction with 'my' group is one of the things that I miss the most since becoming a head of year and then a senior leader. However, it was also challenging at times, with the absence of an accepted safety net, due to registration not being a 'real' lesson and thus potentially lacking focus. I learnt very quickly, from 8NS, that those 20-minute registration sessions were crucial, to them and for me, so I ensured that there was always a structure centred on student-led aspects, as well as a controlled but constructive dialogue between them and me.

The positive and rewarding relationship that you have with your form can be threatened when you are caught in the middle, following negative feedback from colleagues about behaviour of the group (see Class wars and bad groups, page 60) or individuals in lessons in which you were not present. Then you are faced with your tutees pleading their innocence. Your form needs to know that you are ready to support and nurture them. You want them to do well but they must also accept your expectations of them in all their lessons so that they can succeed. This will result in taking time to get beyond the surface and explore the reasons for the manifestation of behaviour, rather than the actual behaviour itself.

I believe that you cannot become an effective teacher unless you strive to become a great form tutor, becoming interested in all that your group does, in lessons and in wider school activities. Remind yourself of why you went into teaching and enjoy a role where the pressure of keeping to schemes of work is off, where the dark marking and assessment clouds do not hang over you, and where you can truly build positive relationships as a result of giving a bit more of yourself than you would have the freedom to, or generally be as comfortable with, in your subject teaching. In fact, once you have become a great form tutor, you can benefit from this confidence in providing pastoral support to students in your classes too – you don't have to be their tutor to show them that you care.

11 A laugh and a smile? Rudeness and disrespect or just embarrassment?

One of the things that would annoy and upset me the most, when I started teaching, was a child smiling or laughing when I was reprimanding them for a minor or more significant misdemeanour. Often I would follow it up, as I tried to rein in my emotions, with a lecture about the utter rudeness and disrespect which had just been displayed, ending with that classic question *'So what is so funny? Share it with everyone, we could all do with a good laugh'*. The incident would pick away at me all day and usually be the focus of a conversation with a colleague where I would talk about the failings of parents to teach proper manners and respect to the youth of the day. The colleague would of course agree, probably because they knew that is what I wanted to hear.

However, on one occasion, a wise teacher interrupted as I was in full flow and asked me to think about whether that student could have been embarrassed or unsure about how to react as I was lambasting them in front of their peers. I immediately rejected this explanation, preferring the easier argument that I had created, as the emotions were still too raw. Later, though, I gave it some more thought and realised that, even though there would be times where the young person in front of me could be displaying rudeness, a much better way to deal with future situations was to talk about embarrassment. Saying *'I am genuinely sorry that I am embarrassing you or putting you on the spot, but I need you to recognise that the impact of how you have chosen to act is ...'* could work better than launching into a boring, tired and mostly ineffective tirade. This change of mindset definitely protected my wellbeing but, most importantly, I realised that having public confrontations was leading to more problems than solutions.

12 Make confrontations a win-win

Everyone makes mistakes, misjudges situations and gets things wrong either deliberately or by accident. The resulting actions by those in charge are crucial in maintaining or building positivity, as well as encouraging a different course of action in the future. It is easy for us to demand sensitivity, respect and patience when adults are in the

CHAPTER 2 **BEST OF THE BEST**

firing line, while dealing with students through firm and accusatory language that lacks the same level of tolerance. It is always important to try to empathise with the students in your class and consider how you would feel and react to public reprimands.

I have delivered staff training sessions where colleagues have been talking or messaging on their phone throughout, a crime that students in my class would be called up on instantly. Yet I was fully aware that making even suggestive comments about this would have immediately damaged the tone and distract attention from the key messages I was trying to deliver. Why this difference in approach? We consider adults to have the maturity and experience to know how to act in certain situations and if they fail then there must be a legitimate acceptable reason, but we do not allow young people the same leniency. Students need to learn and may need help to get to that level. However, anyone, young or old, is likely not to give you the most positive reaction following a public attack which will undoubtedly damage their ego in front of their peers.

We are often advised that a quiet personal chat during or after the lesson will be more effective than a confrontational dressing down. I absolutely agree with this, but it is not always possible to arrange during the flow of your teaching. How can you create a situation where you have to correct poor behaviour with neither you nor your student losing credibility? The language (body and words) you use is key. Rather than telling a student that they *'have'* or *'haven't'*, intimate that you *'are not sure if they understand what you mean'*, *'don't think they wanted to do ...'* or *'cannot see why ...'*. Follow it up with *'It is OK, but ...'*.

A quick reminder: end with a *'thank you'* and then look or walk away from the situation to ensure you don't enter a reputation game which you cannot, but very well might, lose. This is not about students getting away with misdemeanours. You should be clear in your tone while delivering your message with a smile, before carrying on with the lesson in a way that makes it clear to all that you have made both your point and expectations clear but have also given the student time and space to correct themselves, without losing face in front of their public gallery.

13 Simplicity of a three-part lesson

Teaching is a complex art and lessons are full of unpredictable components, so anything that you can do to simplify and bring an element of control over proceedings has to be something desirable.

The basic structure of the three-part lesson provides not only a vital strategy to improve behaviour but also is a model which enables effective learning to take place. Early in my teaching, during a training session on the fashionable new idea of three-part lessons, I remember thinking that I had already decided to teach in this way, but had not formally received training on it before, so had not reflected on the 'why' of this strategy. The beautiful basic lesson can be a godsend, with a starter activity to settle, motivate and engage, followed by a main part consisting of teacher delivery and student practice allowing for quiet working, then finishing with the plenary to reinforce and summarise key learning.

The three-part lesson does not go hand in hand with mundaneness and predictability but provides a helpful structure from where you can launch your creativity. The appetiser should not be limited by time or type of activity, the main course does not always need to be traditional teaching followed by 'working' and the dessert is not a simple matter of Q&A. Choose your tools carefully with consideration given to the class, topic and time.

14 Anagrams – to asrtt and ifshin

We talk about being creative in our teaching but often associated with the planning of different types of learning activities is the dreaded additional workload required. I am certainly not an advocate of spending hours planning for a 60-minute lesson. It is not feasible and is actually not needed. However, teachers sometimes fall victims to a mischievous guilt when they are not planning and marking into the early hours – after all, we do get three months a year 'off' right?

You will work hard as a teacher and some aspects of the job cannot be avoided, yet shortcuts do exist which will not reduce the effectiveness of your lessons but in fact will make you better able to perform in the classroom because you will not be struggling due to a lack of sleep.

CHAPTER 2 **BEST OF THE BEST**

A simple win, which can easily fit into your starters or plenaries, is the use of anagrams. In every area, students need to be familiar with key subject-specific terminology, and anagrams can be an engaging way of introducing this into lessons. The activity could be short and closed or, much better, the anagrams could enable you to open up questioning by expanding on learning around the actual words and therefore reinforce key aspects and assess understanding.

Hwy idd ouy nwta ot eb a chterae?

15 Bad lessons? Blame yourself first

A painful truth that sometimes we need to face as teachers is that, when lessons have not gone well, it is possibly our fault or certainly we played a key role in the failure. To present my argument in a more palatable way, we are the ones who have the most control in terms of fixing the issues.

It is true that student misbehaviour can bring down even the best planned lesson and we have only a limited influence over a young person's mood and resulting acts. However, we have an almost total say over the learning environment and types of activities that make up our lessons. If *you* cannot fix the issues then who will? I have supported teachers who have been aware of this long before any conversation with me. As a result, they started the journey towards excellence much sooner than others who were seemingly unable to disassociate bad lessons with bad students, and therefore saw minimal improvement due to little change to their own practice.

This mindset was summed up nicely by a colleague who used the analogy of refereeing a school rugby fixture and blaming themselves rather than the players when ill-discipline became a barrier to a competitive but enjoyable, free-flowing game. It is important for you to accept this fact, because those around you, in your support bubble (not a reference to Covid!), will most likely echo the idea that you are doing all you can do and it is the students who need to change. They are more likely to tell you what you want to hear, rather than what you need to hear.

16 Slay the marking monster – who is working harder? 15-minute challenge

I have no doubt that every teacher up and down the country has spent late evenings and weekends marking – I certainly have. Unfortunately, it seems that, even with experience, there is no light at the end of this dark and winding tunnel. We again visit the guilt that burdens teachers, this time telling us that marking for hours is an honourable act which will transform us into excellent practitioners. We share our tragic but noble story with colleagues to boost our reputation for being the consummate professional. However, there are ways to make your marking more streamlined without the loss of effective feedback or assessment of understanding.

We'll start this journey by asking some key questions:

- What is the impact of our marking on student learning?

- How much time do we create for students to reflect and act upon our written feedback?

- How much of their written work do we need to mark? What are we trying to achieve?

Too often, I have been guilty of spending a few hours marking and then returning books to students who have had a brief glance at my feedback before moving onto the next topic. The lessons where I have included 15-minute reflection time have sometimes been ineffective, as some students needed little improvement on that task whereas others needed a lot longer than the small portion of the lesson I set aside. I accept that this is mainly down to my own lack of training or specific focus to enable students to use this time effectively.

Peer marking can greatly help reduce your workload but this must be carefully introduced and managed. It takes knowledge and training to be able to provide constructive feedback, yet we can impose this task on our students with minimal guidance and then accept a decent return.

My favourite strategy is to ask students to write a review of their understanding, learning or confidence at the end of each task. To simplify this for them, I just ask for WWW ('What went well') and HTI ('How to improve'). My time is then spent just glancing over their work and responding to their reviews. This was not introduced to reduce workload but to give students greater ownership of their progress, but I quickly found benefits for all once I had taught the class how to review. I persisted with this strategy in the face of initial resistance from students: 'Your homework is not complete unless it has a review'.

So, is it possible to mark a whole set in 15 minutes? Perhaps, but the important thing is to shift one's mindset from hours and hours of marking to much smaller blocks of time. Remember, there will still be learning that needs to be marked thoroughly, but this should be the exception rather than the norm.

17 Slay the planning monster – 10-minute preparation

In our first few years of teaching, the planning monster is an unforgiving and unstoppable beast, but one that we may have unwittingly created ourselves from the outset. Thorough planning is a key feature of excellent practice, yet we do not have the luxury of time to create the perfect lesson. Early in our training, we are welcomed into teaching with a light timetable consisting of one- or two-period days. This is absolutely the right thing to do, given our inexperience, but it can create a false situation that enables hours to be spent planning for each lesson. We quickly need to be encouraged to reduce the time spent preparing, to achieve a more realistic workload. We should also accept that there is no perfect lesson, however much we plan, as a key part of the success is out of our hands and subject to the unpredictability of the classroom. However, the planning monster is not easy to slay until we have developed our strategy, not solely as a result of our gained experience, but by accepting our limitations and experimenting with our approach.

The creation of resources is often referred to as a main factor in the planning challenge, but we must appreciate that in this digital age we are fortunate to have millions of ideas at the click of a button – imagine the envy of our teacher ancestors. However, lurking round the corner is omnipresent guilt and a misguided pride which stops us from using others' ideas for our own gain – now imagine the bemusement of our teacher ancestors. I am not suggesting that we should never plan our own lessons from scratch, as that is an important skill for any teacher, but, by making that approach the norm, we are supplying the monster with vital nutrition to make it an even more powerful foe.

Once teachers have overcome this obstacle, they will have a bank of ideas for a range of lessons that they can deploy with much less effort. **Remember that excellence comes from the delivery, not the planning.** Teachers with leadership roles are sometimes thrust into unexpected situations across the school and as a result have to walk into their lessons with little preparation. Set yourself the 10-minute preparation challenge, initially with a class and a topic you feel comfortable with, then gradually build up confidence to set 10 minutes as the maximum time for planning more of your lessons.

18 Support circles – learn from others

Even though we spend most of our working days surrounded by 20 to 30 young people, teaching can be a lonely profession. In the heat of the moment, we do not have the luxury of pausing lessons and being able to bounce ideas around with colleagues, as we have to respond to situations instantaneously. We have to be our own critical friend, reflecting on the WWW and HTI of our delivery (see Slay the marking monster, page 45) quickly before our brain focuses on the next lesson.

This additional responsibility, placed on us once we have qualified, represents a seismic shift considering the constant feedback and advice we received from experienced teachers in our training year. In addition, we are pushed towards spending significant time observing others. Yet, once we qualify, this vital part of our learning process falls down the list of our priorities, as our energy is consumed with marking, planning and keeping up with administrative tasks. We are supported so much before we achieve qualified teacher status and then the stabilisers are taken off and we are sent speeding down the inclined track. Clearly, our development has not halted and we are in an even more precarious part of our journey, but now we need to take ownership by actively and persistently speaking and listening to others.

CHAPTER 2 **BEST OF THE BEST**

When not in front of a class, surround yourself with a range of colleagues who, irrespective of their experience, skill or subject specialism, will, through light-hearted and informal conversations, enable you to reflect on and absorb key aspects of teaching at a much deeper level than if you travel alone. Staffrooms are not just for having a breaktime coffee!

19 Support staff – the heart and body of the school

While we are often isolated in our own classroom or with our subject departmental colleagues, the busy and beautiful life of the school bubbles away quietly in the background. It can, therefore, be easy to focus solely on teaching, and for teachers to ignore the fundamental impact of the other adults present:

- the army of support staff
- the wisdom and patience of the office and reception team
- the empathy and care of the pastoral and medical team
- the finance team with their organisational skills and knowledge
- the catering team, who build positive relationships with students outside your classroom
- the IT team, who smile through numerous staff complaints about technology while giving tailored support
- the site team whose care for the school may unfortunately go unnoticed, but who have the clearest view of what is going on.

Apologies for generalising, and clearly every adult working in a school will have a range of these skills, but my aim is to highlight the importance of these staff anywhere where they may have faded into the scenery. Schools will organise support staff in different ways, but any educational institution will become significantly less effective without their hard work and ability to focus on matters outside the classroom. Part of your support circle should include these heroes and, as a result, you will benefit from gaining a greater understanding of the whole school, thus increasing your awareness and enhancing your ability to perform your classroom role.

20 Wellbeing – YOU have the power to change the way you view things

As we are thrust into the busy life of a teacher, there will undoubtedly be challenges along the way which test our resolve, both physically and mentally. During their first year, many teachers, including me, will have lost their voice or regularly fallen asleep by 8pm on a Friday evening, as our bodies slowly adjust to the strain of our full-time role. In addition, our mental capacity to deal with a range of factors directly linked to teaching, as well as the impact of our new job on our personal life, is truly tested. I have mentioned the importance of surrounding yourself with others to accompany you on this journey but ultimately you are the one in the driving seat and therefore most responsible for reaching your destination unscathed.

Wellbeing has been an increasingly used term when describing how a school should look after its staff. This has resulted in clear policies and strategies linked to teacher workload and stress, with more visible features such as cakes and biscuits, staffroom facilities and social events. These additions to the working environment are certainly to be welcomed but, for me, wellbeing is a state of mind that each individual should seek to strive for, rather than the imposed feel-good moments that we can enjoy in the short term.

When supporting students who struggle in school, we often work hard to encourage them to focus on the positives, which almost always outweigh the negatives that are so consuming their thinking. We are no different in how easily we convince ourselves that the task we are facing is unmanageable and that we are helplessly subject to factors out of our control. Treat challenging classes as key learning opportunities that you will be grateful for in the future. Treat an increased workload as the necessary evil that forces you to become more focused and efficient in your planning and marking. Consider your lack of confidence as a reminder that this wonderful story is just beginning. I know this is easy for me to say but, by trying to adopt aspects of this positive thinking, you will increase your emotional resilience at a time when it is most needed.

21 Simple messages and instructions repeated over and over

Imagine your annoyance and bemusement if someone repeated the same instructions over and over when asking you to complete a simple task. Surely you only need to be told once or at most twice, if you weren't properly focused initially. Why should it be so different for a teacher explaining functional tasks to students?

Before we judge students too harshly, consider teacher training sessions, which are in many ways similar to being in a classroom. If I reflect on my own experiences of such sessions, distractions, daydreams and not always keeping up with the topic being discussed have sometimes resulted in me whispering to a nearby colleague: *'What are we meant to be doing?'* However, as a teacher, I often felt frustrated when I had (in my opinion) made things clear but still some students seemed to be unaware of my basic instructions and therefore unable to start, making me question their seriousness about learning. Sometimes, I even resorted to the threat of low-level sanctions as a deterrent to their apparently deliberate attempts to derail my lesson. Even with these warnings, the issues did not seem to go away, so I thought that perhaps it stemmed from my lack of clarity. As a result, I accepted defeat and decided to repeat instructions in small chunks several times to such an extent that any onlooker may have thought I was trying to be funny or was resorting to sarcasm.

The impact was instant as I lowered my volume, following the initial run-through of commands. My words not only provided a welcome reminder to those falling behind the pace but also threaded a peaceful and purposeful atmosphere running through the classroom like a calm meditation or subtle hypnosis.

Students are not robots that we program with a series of algorithms. Our instructions are more than just one-offs that serve no wider purpose than informing them about the next stage of a lesson. They can increase engagement and motivation, and improve behaviour when used effectively.

22 Organisation – growing extra arms and legs

Imagine having a tennis training session where your coach is sending balls over the net for you to volley back. As you become more confident, the challenge increases. There is greater variety in the speed and angle, yet you still manage to keep up and send those balls back with a growing air of self-assurance. However, now imagine that three other instructors turn up and also start firing balls at you: one on your left, one on your right and one directly behind you. Which one do you focus on or should you investigate cloning yourself?

Just to achieve the day-to-day tasks of planning, teaching and marking is no mean feat, but what about dealing with emails, remembering staff meetings, department meetings, parents' evenings and report deadlines? There is only one of you. I found that being organised, by writing things down (either with pen and paper or electronically), setting reminders and talking myself through my week were the key tools – or extra arms and legs – that helped me when I felt overwhelmed in my first term of teaching. (It was when I missed my very first report deadline that I realised I could not remember everything.) The pep talk I gave myself each Sunday was my most important extra limb, as I bored myself with the coming week – lessons, assemblies, meetings and deadlines.

My teachers must have assumed that I was a well-organised student, because I never forgot my books or equipment and mainly handed my homework in on time. The truth is that I kept all my books in my heavy bag all the time and rushed to do my homework the day it was set. However, the bag in our teacher brain is not large enough to carry everything that we need to remember, so reminders or mental walkthroughs can reduce this huge task to a point where it is much more manageable. Speaking to students about the importance of being organised will be a regular conversation, so being a role model and sharing your best tips will also be extremely valuable for them.

CHAPTER 2 **BEST OF THE BEST**

Best of the best key takeaways

- ► From the moment you start training, you should seek to identify a list of go-to strategies that are largely failsafe in producing an effective learning environment. A standard three-part lesson, with an engaging starter, will provide you with a simple structure from which you can add more creative learning (not work) activities. Experiment with your safest classes.

- ► Carefully consider which students are succeeding in getting your attention. Do not let the 'good' students lose out by giving more reprimands than praise. Ensure that questioning is inclusive and accessible, but not dominated by the minority. As you seek to succeed through building positive relationships, work hard to get to know your tutor group. Understand the signals that you send out to your students. Remind students about their achievements in your lessons and (importantly) enjoy being in the classroom!

- ► There will be times when you need to challenge the behaviour or attitude of some of your students. It is important to try to understand and empathise with them. No one likes being told off in front of their peers. Make confrontations a win-win by considering your body language and words carefully.

- ► Excellent, experienced teachers understand that they will continue to learn from others around them. Aim to identify what 'works' across your school. Do not isolate yourself in your classroom or your own subject area. Build an understanding of the whole school, gaining insight from all staff – not just teachers.

- ► Teaching can be very difficult, especially in the first few years. Take ownership of your development and be reflective when lessons do not go well. Accept that it may take time to reach a good standard. Set realistic short-term targets to help monitor your progress, including being smarter when planning and marking to help with your workload and wellbeing. Remember that excellence is in the delivery.

CHAPTER 3 **THE POWER STRUGGLE**

Thirty versus one is a battle you simply cannot win if all things are even and both sides play by the same rules – but, remember, you are the teacher and own the conditions of play. However, we know it is anything but straightforward, as students will not just follow a set of imposed demands without questioning and testing the strength of your convictions. This provides the colourful scenery in the background of the classroom picture. Having too many rules and methods to establish control will undoubtedly backfire as you struggle with consistency and students suffer from confusion. Therefore you need to place your strategies in order and decide on the five or six which you will place at the centre of your classroom, and ensure students can remember and adhere to them with relative ease. The power struggle never disappears, however experienced you become, but do not worry – there are many factors in your favour.

CHAPTER 3 **THE POWER STRUGGLE**

23 Your classroom, your rules – seating plan

Schools will have different views on seating plans, ranging from a directive that all classes must have one to, at the other extreme, it being totally at the discretion of the teacher. The *'You can sit where you want'* approach is definitely not one that I would recommend after having fallen foul to it myself when I started teaching and thinking that this would help to build positive relationships. Unfortunately, following this up with *'But if there is a problem then I might have to move you'* is too late and will lead to confrontation about the definition or extent of a 'problem'. When you hear the carefully chosen, innocent student phrase *'I promise I will be good from now on if you don't move me'*; you have already conceded power in an important mini battle.

Putting students in a seating plan is not a negative strategy aimed at destroying friendships. It is a key part of establishing a calm, collaborative and purposeful learning environment. It is important that young people learn to work with their peers. If you do not know your class well enough, seek advice from colleagues about which students with particular needs may benefit from sitting on their own or with selected others. You are in control of changing the dynamic later if you wish, but that is your choice and certainly not something to blackmail students with, as this will lead to the commencement of another game which will end either with you losing or in the role of the unfair villain. You may decide that some classes, for example at sixth form age or in smaller groups, can learn well without the requirement of a seating plan, but let that be your choice. There is also a danger of moving individual students too quickly where random seating has created issues, so plan to reconfigure the whole room at regular intervals. I aim to rearrange seating for each class about once every half term, which allows me to improve or simply vary the dynamic without singling anyone out.

24 A look to say it all

Are you one of those people who can raise one or both eyebrows in a mysterious way or naturally deliver a piercing stare that can cut through an invisible forcefield? No? Me neither, so the ability to get

CHAPTER 3 **THE POWER STRUGGLE**

students on task without speaking has become a skill that I have had to work at to reach even a basic level. It is something that I have found far more effective than making regular short speeches to students about a variety of things, as those invariably end up as mini lectures, slowing the pace of learning. The more you use your voice for the same issue, in a short space of time, the less impact it tends to have in the classroom.

I am not suggesting that 'the look' is foolproof but it does require less effort and is less disruptive to the class. For teachers, the classroom can sometimes feel like playing a game of Whac-A-Mole, as one student after another requires your attention to refocus or for reassurance. Imagine the difference if a stare did the job and you did not need a hammer. Watch experienced teachers deliver looks to praise, to comfort, to motivate, to discourage, to remind or to show disappointment – simple yet magically effective.

As you start experimenting in your classroom, if you do not get the required response then you may need more time to perfect your look. You could be coming across as if you have had too much coffee, are auditioning for the Joker or want to initiate a staring contest. I have lost more than a few such battles to students in my time, just as my eyes start watering!

101 Ways to Win in Teaching in Secondary School

CHAPTER 3 **THE POWER STRUGGLE**

25 Open your door, close their window of opportunity

When teaching a class that you are struggling with, and the noise level is far above what you are comfortable with (despite your best efforts), the natural response, stemming from embarrassment, can be to close the door and hope that nearby colleagues do not hear the chaos. Unfortunately, this puts you further in the position of an isolated teacher lacking not only the tools but, more importantly, the support to improve the situation. The bravery required to keep the classroom door open, perhaps after asking other teachers to come into your lesson if they hear you struggling, should not be underestimated and must be commended. This is not an acceptance of defeat but is equipping you with short-term support that redresses the balance and reminds the class of your persistence in achieving a learning environment with high standards that they will all benefit from.

I would argue that most new teachers will face at least one class which challenges them in this way. Most experienced colleagues will empathise with you, having gone through it themselves, leading them to be more than happy to offer assistance in an understanding way. The classroom door and walls have more importance than just as rectangular slabs – perhaps this is why some innovative schools experimented (both successfully and unsuccessfully) with totally open learning spaces where different groups were taught in the same larger, open area. Imagine how new PE teachers benefit from nearby colleagues when, for example, there are three groups all having lessons next to each other on the school field. It is not only students who can benefit from strength in numbers.

26 Loose control or lose control

Excellent teachers do not operate in a highly controlled, silent and soulless environment where students function like computers who have been programmed and act accordingly. However, they also do not dwell in loud, unruly and chaotic classrooms. The balance achieved will differ from one teacher to another, but the overarching principles will be fixed. Imagine holding a small, injured bird in your hand. If your grip is too tight you will restrict its movements and air, but if your hands do

CHAPTER 3 **THE POWER STRUGGLE**

not provide support and care then it is no better with you than on the floor where you found it. We must decide for ourselves when to insist on some expectations and when to let others go.

Tactically ignoring some behaviours can seriously challenge our notion of rules and required responses, resulting in a different power struggle in our brains. Yet if you decide to pick up on every misdemeanour then your lesson will progress at an inconsistent, but largely slow, pace and you will open yourself up to being the centrepiece in a classroom game of 'now you see me, now you don't'. However, letting more significant misbehaviour pass without challenge will most likely lead to a rapid decline in students' respect for (and confidence in) you. One student whispering to another while you are speaking could be ignored or dealt with by a slight pause and knowing glance, but if such actions continue, you should halt them with a few words, without side-tracking your lesson, before it grows into a bigger threat to your loose control. Yet students calling out answers or speaking over you is on the wrong side of the line and is already disrupting learning, so now you employ firmer control.

27 Sticky note questions

When a nervous new cohort of students starts, we accept that many of the intricacies of a complex school will be alien to them and so we encourage them not to be afraid to ask questions. However, three weeks down the line, the rapid fire of Year 7 queries is halting the progress of your lesson and they are probably taking the initial advice too far, reminding you of when a toddler becomes confident in their speech and wants to learn more about the world around them. You feel slightly trapped, not wanting to curb their welcome enthusiasm but also being aware of the need to largely keep to the objectives of your lesson. In addition, poor listening skills or a possible lack of clarity can lead to students being unaware of instructions. As a result, their questions are met with a groan from others in the class as your patience is tested and you have to choose a measured response. To remedy this, remember the effectiveness of simple messages repeated over and over (see page 50).

CHAPTER 3 **THE POWER STRUGGLE**

In some situations, you may doubt the innocence of your students and suspect an ulterior motive where questions are carefully chosen to derail the lesson, reducing it to nothing more than a long and possibly interesting chat or series of stories. A simple win to release yourself from this mental trap is to distribute sticky notes to the class which can be used by any student who would like to drink from your fountain of knowledge on a relevant topic. These questions can be dealt with whenever you wish, either as you are circulating, as part of a plenary at the end of the lesson, or at the start of the following lesson when you review prior learning.

This simple win is an effective strategy, but like most things in teaching, not a perfect one. Unfortunately, urgent (in their opinion, not yours) questions may need to be asked without delay, as waiting for you to read *'Excuse me, but I really need to go to the toilet'* on a sticky note would not be well received after a messy 'accident'.

28 Don't enjoy the honeymoon too much

The honeymoon period results from students being apprehensive about the unknown but it fades away due to the comfort of familiarity, either within a few lessons or over a period of weeks. Even experienced teachers can be caught out by lowering their guard in the face of a well-behaved and motivated class and then later in the term look back with a tinge of sorrow when the power struggle is not as easy or one-sided any more.

You must approach the honeymoon period as an opportunity that you are lucky to have been given – a chance to establish yourself when the opponent is not quite awake. Use those lessons to create the persona that you want students to remember for the whole year: the commonly used claim in application letters: *'firm but fair'*. By acknowledging that this is a phase and refusing to throw your strategies for establishing good behaviour out of the window (due to a perceived absence of need), you will be able to extend the period and ensure that, when it is over, the marriage will be happy, strong and harmonious for both sides.

CHAPTER 3 **THE POWER STRUGGLE**

Use those precious few weeks to achieve and sustain high standards, picking up on a few specific smaller issues rather than letting things go because the class seems so delightful. **However, be ready to act quickly when the honeymoon is cancelled without your knowledge and the class tries to establish their rules from the start** (see my teaching fail on page 155).

29 No dead time in lessons

The pace and momentum of any lesson is a strong indicator of how successful it will be. Keeping students engaged throughout is the most natural way to establish positive behaviour for learning, rather than trying to strongly enforce your set of rules and be constantly looking for any violations that will require your intervention.

From the moment that students enter your classroom, to the point at which you decide it is time to 'pack up', your task is to keep them thinking with challenging and active learning that sits just outside their comfort zone. This is not so straightforward, especially if you plan lessons that require a great deal of your energy and not so much of your students'. New teachers often talk for too long because that is the portion of the lesson where they feel most in control. Teacher talk and student activity must be well balanced in order to achieve the tempo that is a given for excellent teachers.

Think carefully about how your lesson will look and aim to identify any moments which may appear as 'dead time', perhaps when you are waiting for everyone to arrive, or when resources are being distributed or taken back in. Fill these gaps by planning simple thinking activities that you can quickly follow up on once everyone is 'ready'. Striving for good pace and momentum does not mean that your lessons should run at 100 miles per hour, as students will struggle to cope, and most likely decide to switch off. Instead, aim to travel at a steady speed with minimal stop-start moments that may reverse the progress of the focus and behaviour that you have built.

CHAPTER 3 **THE POWER STRUGGLE**

30 Change 'if you do, then I will' for poor conduct, to 'because you have, now I will' for good behaviour

The language that teachers use, both in terms of words and visual signals, is one of the most important tools for establishing and maintaining good behaviour. It is true to say that planning an engaging and enjoyable lesson can win the initial battle, but students' positivity and desire to learn is topped up by the ongoing messages they hear; otherwise, their enthusiasm will naturally wane as time goes on.

Every school has systems for merits or achievement points, which should be used much more than sanctions. They remind the class that you are more interested in rewarding than punishing. Yet we also know that the effectiveness of such strategies wears off as students get older or if they are given merits too often for suspect or false reasons. If you promise rewards before anything has been earned, you are entering a game where you are suggesting that engagement in learning might only take place in return for a reward. Even worse, individuals can prevent the game progressing at the expense of the class so, to prevent an element of unfairness, you may later change the rules, thereby reducing the legitimacy of the original bargain.

An improved approach and change of emphasis is to reward students after they have deserved recognition. This way, you can construct the rules flexibly and appropriately following the activity, demonstrating that the learning itself is the reward and that your actions are just the resulting recognition of this. You just might be surprised by how effective simple, positive, but meaningful, feedback can be for most students in building respect and trust, without the need for stickers, chocolates or vouchers for the dining hall.

31 Class wars and bad groups

Stating, to yourself or others, that you have a 'bad class' is natural and perfectly understandable when you are finding teaching a group particularly challenging. As a result of either setting or, more often, the mischievous element of randomness, groups can have an unhelpful chemistry that takes its time to form into a positive and cohesive mixture. We accept that, in most classes, it is the norm to have a few students who need more attention but, when you are hit with a much higher proportion of disruptive elements, you lament your fate and speak to friends who offer great sympathy. However, kind words alone do not seem to be enough. You need to seek out others who have similar struggles with that specific group or individuals within it. They will give you the empathy and understanding that you require. Part of the function of your support group is to provide reassurance at these times but be careful that you are not creating a bigger monster in your mind than the tiny ones you have to face in the classroom.

Building a mindset where there are no 'bad classes', just groups that are not quite where you want them yet, is much easier said than done, of course. But if you are able to tell yourself (and your students) that every lesson is a new start and that previous poor behaviour is forgotten, then you can retain control. When your patience is tested, a clear error is to share your feelings with the group that they are *'one of the worst classes you have taught'*. Not only can this be hugely disheartening to the majority who want to do well, but it is also a strong signal to all that you have lost the war and that the disruptive students have the control. Moreover, this news quickly spreads across the school, building unwanted reputations, for the students and for you, that will be difficult to change. Even worse is its potential to alert parents to an issue which suggests that you (as well as the wider school) cannot cope. I have spoken to a number of parents over the years who have been disappointed with the 'bad class' tag and wanted to move their child to different groups or even schools because of minor concerns that almost always improve over time.

Remember to focus on the actions rather than the individuals. I am not suggesting that we bury any truths but, instead, that we acknowledge we are part of that situation and are therefore a key instrument in improving it, by working to change the 'bad class' to a moderate and manageable one and then, eventually, to a good one. This is entirely possible if we do not give up on them.

CHAPTER 3 **THE POWER STRUGGLE**

32 **Elastic band – stretch and relax**

We often refer to 'stretch and challenge' as a vital component of excellent teaching. This means pitching learning at a suitable level which ensures all students can make progress. Sometimes attempts are made to blame poor behaviour, often unfairly and incorrectly, on boredom. Students claim that they find the learning too easy, trying to argue that there was little alternative left than for them to become disruptive. Although I am not an advocate of this explanation, there is clear logic in the argument that the better you engage your students, the more positive their behaviour will be. Challenge can be introduced at the start of a lesson, with an activity carefully designed to sit outside the comfort zone of your students' thinking, yet accessible enough that success is just within their reach. Once you have established the right level, you can continue the lesson with a mixture of key learning that all students should be able to grasp, and activities, often but not always open in nature, that stretch their thinking.

There is an undeniable feel-good factor present whenever we achieve something at a level that we previously considered outside our limitations, especially when that end has been reached through blood, sweat and tears. (Perhaps this is a bit too dramatic, as blood and tears in your class will not end well for you, and sweat could lead to an uncomfortable, whiffy teaching environment, but hopefully you understand my point.) During these moments, remind your class how well they have done as not only will this build their confidence but, more importantly, it will serve as a precious reminder that your class is a place where they enjoy learning, improving and succeeding by working hard.

The elastic band makes a much better 'ping' sound when it is stretched than when it is slack, but your challenge is to find the right ping for your class without going too far. If, while experimenting, the band snaps then do not worry – you can start with a fresh one next lesson.

33 Empathise during tellings-off, don't rant

Do you remember being admonished by your parents, either when you were younger or perhaps even in your adult life? Which tellings-off worked best?

- Being shouted at?
- Being spoken to calmly with clear description and reasoning behind the error of your ways?
- Having to cope with the silent treatment?
- The dreaded *'I am very disappointed'* speech?

We may have differing viewpoints on this, and the actual situation must be taken into account, but in the classroom it is crucial that you remain in control and remember that you are the adult in this situation. Shouting at students is rarely the best option and should be kept for situations where you need attention quickly, due to extreme behaviours or for safety reasons. When I started teaching, I convinced myself that raising my voice to signal my displeasure was a demonstration of my power as a teacher – this is probably why I lost my voice within the first month! Unfortunately for me, when this strategy did not work, I was stuck, as 'the rant' was at the top of my list and I had employed it unnecessarily and far too early.

Shouting is more likely to indicate a loss of control, a lack of ideas and an absence of empathy. Consider the class in front of you and focus on the majority, the 'good kids', as they watch the atmosphere of the lesson drop and your attention is strongly placed on those who are stepping out of line. It is now clear to all who holds the power. The challenge of demonstrating saintly patience is not an easy one. A natural reaction is to shout, as that is a simple way of voicing your annoyance, but a calm response will definitely benefit you in both the short term and for the longer game, as you build mutual respect and a positive relationship with a class over time. Clear tellings-off which start with a *'Let's not …'* or *'It is unfortunate that …'*, with limited emotional input, can make your point quickly and effectively as you refuse to be goaded into a more negative reaction or be sidetracked from the important teaching of your lesson and the large group of students who are already on your side.

CHAPTER 3 **THE POWER STRUGGLE**

34 The power of the start

The power struggle firmly kicks in at the very beginning of your lesson as students arrive from a variety of previous activities, including possibly unhelpful ones such as breaktime, lunchtime or other lessons where calmness may have been lacking. You have a small window of opportunity to establish your control as, often, student behaviour will not deviate much from its starting point, whether that is focused or chaotic. Students coming into your classroom may need a short and stern word to remind them of the levels you expect and will insist on. However, words alone are not enough. You need to consider the learning that you want them to immediately engage in, which will form the basis of their experience over the next hour.

Having an activity ready for them to see as they walk in will direct their energy towards your power and remind them that they are in a lesson they will enjoy, rather than them creating an almost acceptable (in their heads, not yours) five- or ten-minute social time period before **they** decide to start the lesson. The activity could be on their desks, but this may be too time consuming if you consider the creation and distribution of resources. A simple win could be a short but open question on the board that can act as a gateway to your overall learning objective.

35 The power of the plenary

The objective of calming and focusing the class at the start enables you to teach in a positive learning environment but, as your lesson rolls on, student attention will naturally wane. This should be easy to empathise with if you consider your own behaviour towards the end of an hour-long lecture or training session, as your mind wanders and you carefully plan a sneaky look at your watch or phone to reveal just how long is left of your mental torture. (This does not resonate with you? I am not convinced that I believe you!)

The end of your lesson provides an opportunity to re-engage your students as you deepen their understanding and knowledge, but also reaffirms your position as the director of this inclusive, enjoyable and vibrant play all the way to its conclusion. The absence of an effective plenary can see all your hard work in establishing positive behaviour for learning go to waste, as your lesson lacks any direction and the dwindling attention manifests itself into a steadily growing mischievous pest.

Plenaries do not need to be complicated or require a great deal of preparation. They can be very effective in their simplicity and maybe even predictability. Closed questions to test knowledge, teacher-led discussion to tease out future learning or (if you feel more ambitious) a collaborative 'think, pair, share' activity can all subtly remind students of the law of the classroom and, most importantly, be planned on the spot with minimal time and energy required from you.

36 Testing for behaviour

Who does not love a good test? Ranging from short, quick-fire memory recall to longer checks of deeper understanding and, finally, the more significant mocks and formal exams, tests are an accepted aspect of education. Remember the huge controversy in 2020 and 2021, when exams were cancelled and students were awarded the dreaded term 'teacher grades' more accurately, but lesser known as, 'school assessed grades'?

Alongside the clear benefits of assessment of learning to inform future planning and delivery, tests can be a really useful tool to manage classes. They require 'exam conditions' and thus create the behaviour you want, without you having to break into a sweat. Low-stakes, memory-retrieval 'quizzes' (a word which induces more positive emotions than the suspicious and scary term 'test') can be delivered without much planning or disruption to the flow of your teaching and with no need to give students advance warning due to their informal and spot-check nature. However, the rationale and benefits have to be made clear to students. They:

- help both you and them identify strengths and weaknesses
- build confidence over time
- help us better understand our brain's role of storing information
- make revision for larger assessments more manageable
- ultimately, help them succeed in the world of exams.

CHAPTER 3 THE POWER STRUGGLE

I often found that Friday afternoons or windy days prompted me to take this strategy out of my locker. Bear in mind, as with any simple win, overuse will diminish its magic. If it becomes a regular part of your lessons, the low-level chat will start creeping in, so plan its use wisely and in moderation.

37 Don't encourage an audience

As teachers, we know that the numbers game is not in our favour, so we employ a range of strategies to retain control and convince students to work with us, rather than against us. We demonstrate the many benefits of being a collective, yet the young people we teach will often revert back to their peer allegiance if forced to pick sides in an open 'authority versus majority' contest.

When speaking to students, you have a choice about having a public conversation or a 'quiet word'. There are times when you will want to perform to the audience, for example when giving praise, boosting confidence or demonstrating your empathy. However, any open attack on a student's ego during a reprimand is to be avoided wherever possible, as you are tempting the powerful audience to turn on you. A calm one-to-one chat inside the classroom, a quick word after the lesson or asking a student to stand outside during the lesson, so you can speak to them on their own, will often be more effective in reshaping behaviour, demonstrating your humanity through constructive, empathetic dialogue. This helps to build positive relationships – and is much better than a public and embarrassing dressing down delivered in a way that suggests you are not really interested in their story.

Dealing with issues outside the classroom, such as during playground or dining hall duties, can be more of a challenge, as you may feel encircled by larger groups of students. Choosing to speak to individuals in a quieter space, away from the incident, will not only give you time to plan your words but also significantly reduce their desire to argue. There may be situations where you feel you have little choice, and need to deal with a situation immediately or have exhausted other options. By breaking down group resistance with a calming smile, as well as showing some understanding and tolerance, your authority and sense of respect should be left largely unscathed. Remember, not everything can be (or should be) 'dealt with' there and then.

CHAPTER 3 **THE POWER STRUGGLE**

38 Give them space in lessons – they need it

We discussed earlier the benefits of loose control (see page 56), where you enforce rules and maintain standards from a distance without suffocating the positive atmosphere in your classroom. In addition, we must remember to give students time and space to learn, without constantly dominating lessons with our teacher input or tight, constant monitoring.

A trap that new teachers can fall into is talking at the class for too long, thinking that makes behaviour management easier. However, by asking students to be quiet for significant periods, we will eat away at their genuine desire for you to succeed and can quickly encourage them to switch off. (This is natural, of course, if you consider how well you would maintain concentration during a long and largely one-sided conversation or lecture.)

As you become more confident in your ability to manage behaviour, gradually build up to longer periods of student independent or collaborative learning until you get to the point where student activity is a bigger feature of your teaching than basic delivery of knowledge. Your impact as a teacher will come through effective circulating and monitoring, where you challenge thinking by asking deeper questions, refining or correcting their ideas and offering support for those who need to build greater resilience, while continuing to enforce behaviour expectations with a light touch.

Get to know your classes, as each will require a different balance of teacher talk and student activity – both of which are crucial to the effective learning of subject content, as well as developing skills and character.

39 Ownership of the line

Clearly, different types of classroom activities will require variation and flexibility in your expectations for behaviour. Silent group work might encourage students to develop their non-verbal communication skills (and could provide some humour as you watch from the sidelines!) but will not result in the effective learning that you are looking for. Yet you need a quiet environment during traditional teacher delivery

CHAPTER 3 THE POWER STRUGGLE

and, in between these two, we can use paired activities which require talking but not at a level where the students cannot hear or be heard themselves.

Flexibility should also exist when we consider our classes, with the approach to sixth form or small groups perhaps noticeably different to younger students or groups where control has not fully been established. In addition, we might set different standards for the same group across the week, with the knowledge that what we can expect on a Monday morning is not going to be identical to our other lessons with them. Does this create an issue due to a lack of consistency? I would argue no – as long as you stick to your key principles and non-negotiables, such as no talking when you are talking, no shouting across the class and everyone acting with mutual respect.

The line is yours to own and to draw, how and where you want. Understand that our wonderfully human and not boringly robotic students will naturally push boundaries and you will rightly resist changing your line. However, at times you may find that it would be wise to alter your line where appropriate, based on the non-verbal informal feedback and reactions from your audience. The struggle for control can easily be lost if the position of the line is unrealistic and your stubbornness is preventing you from redrawing it.

40 Write the following down

The first few minutes of any lesson are crucial in the power struggle, as you need to establish dominance quickly without losing your temper, which would blow a cloud of negativity across the room and usurp the engaging and inclusive learning environment that you seek to create. Once we gain experience or build relationships with a class, the students know what to expect and will enter the classroom largely in the right manner, leaving observers bemused by the apparent invisible mind control – remember watching experienced teachers getting a class quiet with seemingly minimal effort? However, until we reach that point, we need simple wins that give us the upper hand in settling a class down at the start of a lesson. Just asking a class to be quiet will produce inconsistent results. By varying our instructions to deliver different types of subconscious messages (see 'Stand up, sit down', page 39), we can find strategies that will work with classes most of the time.

CHAPTER 3 **THE POWER STRUGGLE**

The simplicity of asking students to write something down can hurry them into action and redirect their focus from their peers to you and their learning. Consider the difference in tone between the pleading and begging for silence: *'Will you please be quiet?'*, as opposed to the demanding but also encouraging words: *'Come on, hurry up, write this down, we need to start the lesson, well done to those of you who have already ...'*.

Ensure that some type of activity quickly follows; otherwise, students who are already engaged and have completed the dictation without being asked several times will have dead time that they need to fill. This basic task of students listening to you and copying down your words does not need to be long and is not crucial to their learning but is designed to settle and quieten, so that they can focus on your teaching.

41 **De-escalate**

I can remember having numerous conversations with students who succumbed to poor behaviour too easily when provoked about the need to remove themselves from a situation, count to 10 and develop greater empathy or better understand the challenges of others. This can be a long journey for them but is, of course, an important life skill. Until they are better trained, some young people can react quite instinctively and without consideration of consequences during interactions with either their peers or the adults who are trying to support them. Even excellent teachers, who have gained the utmost respect from students and maintain high levels of classroom behaviour, will find themselves in situations where students are directly challenging authority. This is often out of character or sometimes (unfortunately) is part of their approach to life and school at that given time, due to factors out of our control.

As teachers, we protect ourselves with rules and accepted hierarchy but what happens when the student you are faced with does not appear bothered and willingly steps out of line without fear of repercussions? If we continue playing the same *'I am the teacher and you are the student, so will do what I ask'* game then we are doomed to failure, at least in that instant. The young person in question will need to face more senior members of staff anyway if they are being

CHAPTER 3 **THE POWER STRUGGLE**

openly defiant. During these moments, your ability to de-escalate the situation will certainly be an important tactic in the power struggle. Do not consider this as giving in to students with challenging behaviour, but as more a demonstration of how you can stay in control and maintain composure in the face of provocation.

Unlike the students I referred to earlier, you cannot take yourself out of the situation, do not need to count to 10 and have a developed skill of empathy, but the language and tone of your response can exude patience and authority at the same time. Calm phrases, said with genuine care, can be very effective in de-escalating and therefore supporting the students, but not at the expense of your reputation. For example:

- *'I am sorry that you feel that way but ...'*

- *'I can see you are not yourself, but that behaviour is not acceptable'*

- *'It is interesting that you think that and I can see why, but ...'*

- *'I really want to work with you, so can you/are you able to ...'.*

Remember the need for the line you draw to be flexible. Accept that sometimes your authority alone will not be enough and therefore your emotional intelligence can be a vital tool that will disarm without drama or emotional reactions on either side.

The power struggle key takeaways

- Getting students to behave in the classroom will most likely be the biggest challenge that new teachers face. Do not overcomplicate your rules and expectations. Seek to build your practice around five or six key strategies, some of which can be in place before any lesson starts, such as a non-negotiable seating plan for all your classes.

- We need students on our side – after all, the large majority will want to learn and do well. Develop positive relationships by establishing a good balance between control and limited freedoms; you get to decide where your line is. Your actions will back this up – body language and choice of words when both praising and reprimanding are the keys to success or failure.

- Understand that all teachers will have faced challenges with establishing classroom control at some point. Do not isolate yourself by closing your door and pretending that everything is fine. Seek help and learn from others around you rather than just accepting that you cannot do anything with the 'bad class'.

- Good habits for behaviour can be established if learning is regularly engaging and suitably challenging. From the start to the end of a lesson, students should be made to think – effective starters and plenaries do not need to be overly complicated. Periods of 'dead' time should be avoided when planning.

- Use the honeymoon period to your advantage by setting and maintaining high expectations for longer. Behaviour of classes may decline after the first few weeks so consider how you deal with numerous student questions, as well as the place that rewards have in your teaching. Remember that praise and merits are just the recognition of success, not the ultimate goal.

CHAPTER 4
THE HUMAN TOUCH

Wars, battles, weapons, power and control – is this what you went into teaching for? My words may have alarmed you and painted a darker picture of the life of a teacher than intended, but, as I stated earlier, this is a vocation which gives me immense enjoyment and fulfilment every single day. It is easy to become fixated on scenarios where our patience and mental resilience are tested, as we find ourselves dealing with poor behaviour and a lack of motivation from our students. There are times when we do need to resort to 'bad cop' mode but usually the most effective strategy – aimed at establishing a learning environment where all can thrive – is positive behaviour management, which places

CHAPTER 4 **THE HUMAN TOUCH**

support, reward and recognition far above threats, reprimands and sanctions. Prevention is better than cure, as Erasmus reminded us over 500 years ago. Reflect on the reasons why teaching attracted you so much and led you to enter such a challenging profession. Hopefully, it was the thrill of working with young people and having a positive impact on their lives, more than the salary, holidays and authority.

How easy do you find it to reflect on your own experience of being in the classroom? Take yourself to that dark place in your past where you were a young person who the current you would probably not want to teach. Consider the reasons for your actions. Were they always born out of rationality and logic, or were they sometimes chaotic, impulsive and inconsistent? You may honestly remember no such past behaviours and might need to gain insight from others or watch films or clips of 'naughty children' in the classroom, such as the wonderfully funny but also uncomfortably accurate Catherine Tate 'Lauren Cooper' sketches. I have plenty of moments to draw on myself, even as a (mostly) well-behaved and bright student.

We need a great deal of empathy for young people so that we can make reasonable allowances in the classroom, appreciating the possibility of numerous challenges outside our gaze that may manifest in the behaviours in our lesson. It is natural to have a bad day or to make poor choices, but remember you are the adult in the situation and can use your experience and insight to prevent the escalation of issues. Understanding that you need to be flexible in your teaching is not leaving yourself open to the lowering of standards. It simply makes you better at reacting to inevitable situations with humanity and care rather than coldness and indifference.

It is natural to dream about classes where students follow your instructions without question or delay. However, not only would teaching become the most tedious of professions, boring you day after day, it would also prevent any development of personality, learning skills or character in the precious young people in your care. Excellent teachers are warm, caring and friendly human beings first and learning tourist guides after. Above all, your ability to inspire and create a passion for learning in your students is far more important than being a firm disciplinarian who runs a tight ship. Hearts and minds.

42 Build lessons around what they need and want (and tell them what they want if they don't know)

Schemes of work (more aptly and fashionably known as schemes of learning) act as your instruction manuals for lesson planning. Even if there is some flexibility in your setting, there has to be an element of rigidness in what you are expected to teach over a week, fortnight and half-term period – otherwise, your class will not cover the key learning that has been decided for them. However, the most important consideration when planning is your customers: the abilities, interests and needs of your students.

To combat students saying, *'Why do we need to learn this and when will we ever use this?'*, I have taught algebra in a variety of ways and using different reference points, ranging from sport, music, language and social media. I am convinced that any topic in any subject can be brought to life for students in a way that will resonate with, and therefore further engage, them. Remember that much of what you teach will not be explicitly used by most students in their future lives, so it is in the development of their skills and character where you will have the biggest impact.

Effectively adapting your planning to suit your students does require you to understand their backgrounds, interests and needs, and this should be your habitual approach, rather than viewing it as an unwanted dilution of the protected chemical mixture that you 'have to' teach. We know that students make better progress when learning is more meaningful and that the 'memory palace' which enables us to retain knowledge operates in areas of our brain which contain previously stored information. Therefore, it is obvious that excellent practitioners understand and teach to the students in front of them, altering their approach from one class to another, but constantly informing them of the significance of the learning both from an education and a life viewpoint.

If you start to panic about the additional planning time this will require, set yourself the challenge of planning a lesson (or, at first, a starter) in just 10 minutes for a topic which might be your algebra equivalent. Repeat this every week or so as you review and develop learning activities better suited to your students.

43 'Yes, Sir', 'Yes, Miss' and the disarming smile

Displaying your friendly and positive human side does not turn you into the easy touch that we are all so wary of and are so keen to avoid. We can draw from our past and recollect the chaos inside the classroom of 'nice', but maybe too nice, teachers who were unable or seemed unwilling to exert authority with any real success. Yet we should also remember our favourite teachers who displayed positivity and clearly enjoyed being in the classroom, at the same time as having the steel to act swiftly on the odd occasion that students wanted to test patience and resolve, without shouting or losing their cool. When verbal reprimands are short, to the point and constructive, they are less likely to cause resentment from the recipient or ruin the enjoyable flow of the lesson.

The disarming nature of a genuine, warm smile is not to be underestimated. There is much scientific research telling us of the vast benefits, for both parties, to our wellbeing and to help create positive relationships. If you feel that the situation merits more than just a pleasant telling off, then end by asking your student *'Is that OK?'* Most will say yes, because you have treated them with respect, and, when they do respond, ask them to repeat with a *'Yes, Sir'* or *'Yes, Miss'*, not to undermine the retreat that they have just made, but to reaffirm it.

You have clearly cast yourself as the authority figure but also enhanced your profile as a fair and approachable teacher. There will be situations, after repeated issues, where you do need to show false annoyance and some students who will resent bowing down publicly, but the majority of low-level issues can be flicked away gently, like the eyelash that is slightly impeding your vision.

CHAPTER 4 **THE HUMAN TOUCH**

44 **Name that name**

'I'm no good at remembering names.' For the first few years of my teaching career, this was something that I had convinced myself of, conveniently moving this crucial task lower and lower down my priorities to the point where it would take me maybe a whole term to learn names of students that I would see three times a week.

I am now slightly embarrassed to share my previous apathy, especially considering my own annoyance when the name Gurdeep, or Mr Singh, has been too difficult for others to remember or indeed spell. (Having said that, 'Mr Zinger' does have a certain spark about it!)

The challenge of learning a few hundred names each year is a significant one and that is the reason why we must spend time retaining those vital pieces of information, exploring methods that are effective for each of us. Visual seating plans, using memory palace stories or simple rote learning are the most common strategies, but these must be backed up with continual practice, either in the classroom or around the school when you follow up the uplifting *'Good morning'* with the right name.

In the same way that a smile has a magic effect, using a name can create positivity, boost confidence and build respect, as you show your students that you are interested and invested in them beyond simply requiring them to do the work that you set. You might take the time to learn, and be more successful with, shorter or easier names, but mispronunciation can undermine your efforts, so seek out the phonetic breakdown where needed. In my first year of teaching, I remember my pitiful attempts with the name Siobhan and her saintly patience and understanding. Students are more likely to respond quickly and correctly when the teacher in front of them seems to have the upper hand, due to the power of knowing their name, and it would be foolish for any teacher not to take advantage of this fact.

45 **Good detentions**

Detentions – the word alone fills new secondary students with dread as stories are shared about the mysterious and torturous activities that are dished out to those unfortunate enough to be given one. Senior students convince the younger ones that detentions are sometimes given for getting lost and turning up late for lessons or just for innocently smiling in front of the wrong teacher at the wrong time. As they get older, detentions have a badge of honour status, with reputations built around how many can be collected in a short time.

Finally, they are met with apathy by students who have faced the worst that can be given and lived to tell the tale, over and over.

For teachers, detentions can be our go-to threat when all the niceties have run their course and we are forced to demonstrate that we mean business and are not negotiating the position of our line. However, once detentions alone become ineffective, when we see the same students regularly attending our lunchtime or after-school compulsory clubs (with them appearing to have a season ticket), we definitely need to consider their purpose.

Obviously, detentions are deterrents for misbehaviour that should force any student to review and change their approach accordingly, but they are also a precious opportunity for calm and constructive conversations without an audience. Rather than zero engagement between both parties during the punishment, use the time for one-to-one discussions to better understand the reasons behind their misbehaviour and to inform the student about the impact of those actions on you and the rest of the class. Have an open dialogue that enables both you and the student in question to work together more positively in the future. It might take time to have an impact but persevere, as change might be more gradual than immediate.

Use the human touch to demonstrate that you have not taken things personally and that your ultimate goal is seeing the student in front of you happier and more successful in their learning.

46 Praise for everyone

Do you remember the uplifting and energising internal glow that you carried around after being the recipient of positive, sincere and personal feedback? You may have not known how to respond and gave little away in your body language, but you could not contain the inner pride as you fulfilled the subconscious desire we all have to please and

CHAPTER 4 **THE HUMAN TOUCH**

be appreciated by others. Being given recognition naturally impacts our motivation as we develop a taste for this wonderful buzz and seek it out more and more.

Use this very effective tool in your teaching, as even the most apathetic, hardened and apparently negative student will respond favourably to praise, whether or not they show it. However, we must carefully consider the nature of our words and the arena in which we deliver them, as we do not want to create a scenario where any student becomes sceptical or fearful when receiving praise and then acts to deliberately avoid it.

Dishing out positive feedback when it is not fully deserved is a common mistake when dealing with the most challenging students, as it further enhances their power in the classroom when they get a better deal than everyone else. Praise must be genuine and your distribution of it must be seen to be fair, but we must also seek opportunities to recognise students in situations where our focus steers dangerously towards the negatives. As we learn more about our classes, we are able to judge which students would welcome public praise and which would view it as open shaming. A more effective approach might be the quiet word during the lesson or, my favourite, to keep the student briefly after class and as they are racking their brains for what they did wrong, you tell them how impressed you were with their effort and attitude – a truly simple win!

Avoid the trap of only praising the brightest or most hardworking students and remember that no one is undeserving of your attention and recognition.

47 Give a little piece of your heart

Based on their initial shock when they see me out with my family, shopping or socialising, I would suggest some students may doubt that their teachers actually exist outside the classroom. In their eyes, perhaps our sole function in life is to deliver lessons and be seen around the school and, as soon as the bell goes at the end of the day, we enter hibernation until the following morning.

Just as we should not consider young people to be clones ready to be programmed, we need to demonstrate that we are not cold and uncompromising robots. Demonstrating our vulnerable and imperfect human side in front of a class is something that we might naturally approach with anxiety and scepticism. I am certainly not advocating a 'laying all out to bare' approach, but sharing part of your own journey with students can be an effective way of establishing positive relationships and building mutual respect.

Our role as classroom teachers is far beyond just delivering subject content. We nurture and aid the development of the young people in our care and they can learn at a deeper level if they see purpose, relevance and reality. Consider the bizarreness of bringing up a child without sharing your own story, life lessons and associated gems of knowledge. I have become quite comfortable talking about my family or my past during assemblies, lessons and pastoral conversations, as I seek to project the importance of honesty, self-reflection and learning from mistakes – but not so much that I risk losing my useful shield of mystery and intrigue. Give snippets of yourself only where it enhances learning and in moderation, as not only might your authority be undermined, interest will probably wane, risking damaging your ego.

48 'I haven't got a pen'

As teachers we all have our own bugbears and frustrations that we can find difficult to rise above or escape from. Students turning up to lessons with no equipment is one of mine that has slightly diminished over time but still evokes an emotional reaction.

I remember dishing out numerous lectures about the importance of organisation and the recipe for success, ending with the *'Do not turn up to my lesson again without a pen!'* threat. It had little impact on some students, who would force me to go through the same speech the following lesson. Occasionally, my patience would be truly tested by a brave soul responding to my rant with the counter threat of *'I haven't got a pen so can't do any work until you give me one.'* I can smile now, but I definitely did not then!

CHAPTER 4 **THE HUMAN TOUCH**

As I was airing my grievances to a colleague, I was aghast at her response – she simply lent out equipment and did not see why I appeared so intent on creating an issue for students who might have had much more important things going on in their lives than worrying about the contents of a non-existent pencil case. I kept my disapproval inside. Reflecting with embarrassment, at some point later, I realised that some of my lessons started on a negative note when a low-level issue became a significant incident, due solely to a choice I had made.

After seeing the error of my ways, the positive impact on lessons was immediate. My strategy changed to having a bank of equipment available or calmly asking if items could be borrowed from another student, with manners and politeness taking over, encouraging them to show gratitude and appreciation where required.

Repeated issues can be followed up, if needed, with parents or pastoral staff after lessons without impacting on the learning for any student. Interestingly, I also use this approach in staff training, as teachers are not exempt from this horrendous crime – how often have you attended external CPD when pens have not been neatly laid out on the table?

Your bugbears do help you retain standards that you are comfortable with, but if they are fed too much, or too often, then they can become domineering and unhelpful, so be careful.

49 Calming of the mind

We have already discussed the importance of a clear learning focus at the start of lessons. We also stated that, without establishing good levels of behaviour, our best intentions are doomed to failure. Now let's consider the racing thoughts flying and bouncing around in the minds of our young people as they navigate a school day full of interactions, conversations and other auditory and visual stimuli. Yet we demand their undivided attention. Perhaps we should not expect them to be able to switch off distractions in their brain so easily – we have a responsibility to support them in this challenge.

Deep breathing, relaxing music and calm, hypnotic instructions from you, maybe with the addition of them closing their eyes, could be viewed as the actions of a zany teacher who does not understand young people and will undoubtedly face ridicule and failure. However, if you balance this sceptical response with the many accepted benefits of meditation – such as management of stress, improved self-awareness, reduced negativity and increased imagination, creativity, patience and tolerance – you begin to wonder why such an approach has not been a fundamental aspect of the start of every lesson. As we predict the initial resistance from students, we can also imagine the benefits to our lesson when classes are trained and fully accepting of a 'trick' which improves them as they become happier and self-aware learners, making your teaching far more effective.

As with any simple win, choose your lessons and classes carefully as you start to experiment and develop an approach that you are comfortable with before you roll out to other more challenging groups.

50 Excuse me, am I boring you?

Have you ever sat in a training session and happily drifted away, thinking about more interesting aspects of your life, blaming your poor conduct on the lack of excitement that learning about (for example) data protection, brings? If your answer is no, then ask yourself the question again until you give an honest answer – otherwise, you are truly a saint or part of a new line of friendly Terminators or Robocops.

Our attention span is not infinite and, even with the best intentions, about 20 minutes is all that we are capable of concentrating for. This is a prime reason for teacher talk not being a dominant feature of lessons. Indeed, 20 minutes may be calculated on the assumption that we are learning about something which interests us. If we accept that not all our young people share our passion and motivation for our subject, an uncomfortable truth to face is that we will be boring some of our students some of the time.

Given students' acting skills, their boredom could go under our radar or, in contrast, be blindingly obvious with a stare out of the window, a head on the desk or a worrying fixation on a dull piece of their stationery. As you spot the switching-off student, I suggest that you

CHAPTER 4 **THE HUMAN TOUCH**

show empathy with an understanding and calm reminder, rather than berating them for demonstrating a natural human response. This does not suggest a lowering of standards but more the clearing of a path for them so that they can walk more positively to meet you at your line. A simple *'Excuse me, am I boring you? I am sorry, I must try better'*, said with a smile can be much more effective than a stern *'What is so interesting out there that is more important than my lesson?'* They might just tell you – not to be defiant, but because it is their truth.

51 The pat on the back

Remember that you are doing a good job which is much appreciated. The human touch should not be solely focused on your students and the different strategies to motivate, praise and support them – what about giving yourself that sorely needed uplift? Teaching can be a challenging profession with the rewards not always obvious, explicit or so visible. Our energy zaps away during the term and we can gradually lose sight of the important and valuable role that we play. Unfortunately, there is limited recognition of this in the media, with a blame culture that springs into action when perceived mistakes or failures occur. Lazy and ungrateful teachers we are not! School leadership may provide positive feedback but it's on a more general and whole staff level, so we might crave more regular, individual, glowing and heartfelt statements on our performance that are sadly absent. Effective mentors give us the boost that we require when we start teaching, but after a few years we are on our own. We have a key role to play to plug this gap, yet, for most of us, it is not in our nature to congratulate ourselves, as we are cautious of arrogance or are blinded to our own achievements.

I learnt early on to save any letters or emails from parents and students who thanked me for the difference I was making. Wine or boxes of chocolates at the end of term are very welcome, but they do not stand the test of time so well. As we face that self-doubt which we adamantly hide from others, or need the praise to motivate us during exhausting weeks, we can return to those words which provide us with essential energy and much-needed reminders. Moreover, make your collection of feedback essential reading in the last week of the summer break, as you wonder whether you will actually remember how to teach.

52 Getting it wrong and changing your mind

It is unfair for any person or group to be subjected to expectations of perfection and the pressure of never getting things wrong. Consider the impact and repercussions of mistakes by health professionals, police officers and others who serve the public, and it is easy to see why denials or the switching of blame can unfortunately be common responses. The pressure on teachers is much lower but not insignificant, as we are faced with 30 young people who look to us for faultless knowledge, guidance and on-the-spot decision making. However, we must also remember that our students need role models who can demonstrate positive reactions to the challenges that we all face, such as failure and mistakes.

Early in my career, I remember students who challenged my limited knowledge, situations where my basic maths skills let me down, the classic mind blank and my subsequent panic, and thoughts of having 'lost the class'. I feel that I was judged more on my reactions rather than my actual 'mistakes'. In addition, I felt bound by anything I had said to a class, treating comments as promises that could not be broken. Once I reduced the pressure on myself and felt more of an urge to talk through my mistakes and limitations, then, undoubtedly, I took another step towards being a better teacher.

Students do not expect perfection from you. Instead, they value honesty. Demonstrating (or if you would rather, accepting) your flaws and limitations enables students to connect with you and learn from your reactions. Getting it wrong sometimes or changing your mind when you see a better option are natural parts of life and should be discussed with students alongside the taking of measured risks, as a valuable exploration into learning and developing. Eating humble pie is more palatable than begrudgingly and reluctantly eating your words.

CHAPTER 4 **THE HUMAN TOUCH**

53 Am I doing a good job? What could I change?

Picture this scenario. It's the end of an enjoyable, interesting and engaging professional development day, away from school. You are tired, thinking about the upcoming journey and whether you will be able to make the 16:30 train that will result in you getting home at a decent time, when your worst fear comes true: the appearance of the 'short' feedback form, resulting in mild panic. I have lost count of the number of times I have been asked for my feedback, at the end of a course, after purchasing some type of service or buying anything online. Should I be totally honest and therefore enter a longer dialogue, or give very short and positive responses to end the questioning in a few minutes?

For teachers, 'customer' feedback can be invaluable, but first we need to overcome the fear and scepticism about what our students might say about our lessons – and therefore about our quality as a teacher and maybe even as a person. However, we should accept that no other group, including you, your colleagues, school leadership, Ofsted inspectors, governors or parents are better positioned to be able to inform you of the effectiveness of your teaching on their learning. Carefully consider what you ask, as opting for open-style questions such as *'What could I do to make lessons better?'* is more likely to lead to requests for more videos, trips, games and **fun** activities. Far more beneficial would be to ask specific probing questions, such as *'Did that activity help you to learn the key aspect and what did you find most useful and why?'*. In my experience, students give honest but constructive and sensitive feedback and this has been vital to improving my teaching. By acknowledging and responding to the most useful aspects of it, I have been able to demonstrate the genuine partnership with young people that I value (and supports me) in my classroom.

54 Meet and greet

What is the first interaction you have with students when they walk into your classroom? I remember having to attend a speed awareness course on a precious, sunny Saturday morning, with negativity, embarrassment and cynicism running wildly through my veins. However, I was almost entirely disarmed by the genuine, personal and positive greeting I received as soon as I entered the makeshift learning space. I am not saying that I greatly enjoyed the day, but my attitude and approach to the learning ahead certainly improved and I felt more desire to meaningfully engage. I contrast that experience and the impact on my mindset with other situations where I have felt mostly invisible, sometimes uncomfortable or occasionally unwanted when entering a new environment.

To warmly welcome your students into your classroom is, of course, a basic concept, yet in the rush of a teaching day we can be too busy in preparing the activities or visual prompts and then waste a vital opportunity to share a warm greeting and uplifting smile, which can only have a positive impact on the lesson ahead. I am not a fan of greeting every single student with a *'Good morning!'* as I think it is unrealistic and can come across as staged and something teachers do because they feel they should. However, *'Come in, it is really good to see you all!'* with maybe a few positive words for selected individuals can be more natural while still retaining the feel of a personal greeting. It reminds students that they are wanted in your classroom and, despite any challenges, you enjoy teaching them. Even latecomers should receive the same greeting regardless of any questions you may need to ask about their punctuality. Often subtle, subconscious messages are the most effective to demonstrate your human side.

55 The new student

Speaking from personal experience, being the 'new student' in a secondary school can be an uncomfortable and lonely time, as you are surrounded by a powerful level of familiarity and trust from which you are temporarily excluded. Other students may initially approach you with caution. You may have not yet developed the skills to enter new situations with confidence but are focused more on the potential long-term ramifications of saying the wrong thing or making the wrong move. You just want to keep your head down until attention and interest shifts to something else. At the same time, you view teachers as the one source of reassurance and safety that you should be able to rely on, but what signals are being sent from them? Is it annoyance that they were unaware of your arrival, are they wondering if there are enough resources or maybe there are small signs of frustration that the seating plan is going to have to be updated? Does the new student largely go under the radar with a simple *'Come in and you can sit there'*? Or perhaps you ask them to tell the class about themselves? This can occasionally work well, but must be very, *very* carefully managed.

Consider how we support new staff through a range of different formal and informal mechanisms. Remember that new students need simultaneous recognition and protective invisibility – they do not want to be 'new' but cannot escape the fact that they need buddies and chaperones to survive the first few weeks. You can make an effort to reassure them through a safe, quick, empathetic, welcoming chat at the end of a lesson, rather than in full view of the gallery. Just be aware that you may need to ask another student to wait outside so that the newbie does not face an unknown journey to their next destination, further adding to their already challenging first few days! New students, including arrivals in the sixth form, cannot just be 'dropped' into the school and expected to get on with it. Although these students will inevitably swim, rather than sink, support from teachers will definitely make the experience more positive and the transition period smoother.

56 Parents – emails and phone calls

In the hectic life of being a teacher, unfortunately we often prioritise parental communication to follow up on poor conduct over providing positive feedback. In order to aid the improvement of behaviour over time, both types of conversations with home are important but can have contrasting effects on our wellbeing, as well as how we are perceived.

When seeking support from parents where a student fails to meet expectations, you must carefully consider at what point communication is initiated. Early action (or when issues could still be viewed as minor) may indicate a lack of control or that you have tried a limited number of strategies, perhaps enabling the student to convince their parents that the real issue is actually you. However, leaving the situation to deteriorate to a point where behaviour is significantly poor will lead to frustration from parents, who might make conversations difficult as they challenge you about your decision to not involve them earlier.

As your time becomes squeezed, do also aim to contact parents of students who have consistently impressed you with their approach to learning, or even those who go under the radar but deserve praise for their consistent effort and attitude. Remember to reflect on who is ahead in the battle for your attention and ask yourself whether the 'good kids' are winning. Having conversations of a positive nature will give you (and them) a psychological boost and enhance your reputation as an effective teacher who truly cares about and enjoys teaching their students.

Every school will have formal systems of reward, including reporting mechanisms and parents' evenings, but we know that the personal touch can be so much more effective – which is why it is more in our minds when student behaviour challenges us. As you become more in tune with parents, you can judge the effectiveness of an email compared to a phone call, but a starting point could be sending an initial email with an offer of a follow up conversation for students with poor conduct, and a phone call for positive recognition – either way, parents will appreciate you taking the time. I have worked with excellent colleagues who would take time at the end of each busy week to phone one or two parents of hardworking students and thus enter the weekend with a reminder of the difference that they are making. There will be situations where parents are not especially supportive or interested, but these will definitely be the minority and even in these cases there have been benefits to my teaching and wellbeing following contacting home.

CHAPTER 4 **THE HUMAN TOUCH**

The human touch key takeaways

- ▶ Dealing with students in a positive manner is almost always far more effective than resorting to tellings-off, which could appear to suggest a lack of empathy and understanding from you.

- ▶ Establish positive relationships with your students. Get to know them, learn their names and aim to establish a link with each of them. This is especially important for students who are challenging, students who are quiet and students new to your class.

- ▶ All of us thrive on receiving genuine and heartfelt praise but, for some students, this might be better received via a quiet word than in public view. Make sure that your recognition covers all students, not just the 'brightest' or most hardworking. Acknowledge improvements made by students where there have been issues.

- ▶ Sharing positive feedback with parents enhances relationships in the classroom, but is also a useful way of supporting your wellbeing and reminding you of the impact that you are having on your classes. Do not forget to be kind to (and praise) yourself!

- ▶ Teachers are human and do not need to be perfect. You can role model dealing with mistakes, being reflective or changing your mind for your students. Be brave enough to include student voice in the feedback process, in order to make your teaching better.

CHAPTER 5 **WALK THE WALK**

What does an excellent teacher 'look' like? Why do some new teachers seemingly command respect upon entering the classroom, yet for others it can take years? If you were to design the perfect teacher, what importance would you place on their appearance, how they sound, their emotional intelligence, their subject knowledge, age, experience, interests ...? The list of possible ingredients can go on.

The beauty of the teaching profession is that excellence comes in a variety of forms, with key aspects being a mixture of traits that form our genetic makeup, our personality and other elements that can certainly be taught and developed over time. Exuding confidence in front of classes and colleagues is a must. Appearing self-assured will build respect, which is then followed up by our actions – but we must be aware that how we 'perform' outside the classroom is equally important as our delivery in lessons. You want to be taken seriously and, fortunately, you have the greatest influence on how others perceive you. Take advantage of that fact.

57 Dress as a role model

Opinions are formed immediately and despite the widely accepted notion of not judging a book by its cover, we also accept that 'first impressions last' and thus we cannot escape the fact that our appearance really does matter. I am not referring to gender, race, height, hair colour or style, weight or other physical features, but more the way in which we choose to present ourselves. In the formal setting of a school environment, teachers are held up, rightly, as role models, and the ones who should set the tone for everyone else in the way they behave, the language they use, the decisions they make and, of course, their appearance.

The importance of individuality is an important message that students need to hear, but this sits under a loose banner of uniformity. Although we should not require teachers to appear as clones, they must portray themselves as clearly belonging in the school environment in order to be respected as educators of hearts and minds. Schools may differ in their requirements for staff, but it's key for you to be clear about your own expectations of yourself in order to be viewed as a role model, before even gracing your students with your teaching. By making the effort, you will demonstrate the importance that you place on your professionalism and your desire to do the best for your students.

There will be a chance to let your hair down and show your casual style, such as on non-uniform days or trips, as your students remember that you do exist outside of teaching, and you will be amused by their reactions (which are not so expertly hidden) to your 'trendy' look.

58 Good morning, good morning

We discussed earlier the benefits, for all parties, of greeting and welcoming students at the start of lessons and acknowledging their departure as they leave, but as you walk the walk around the school, consider how you interact with anyone you come across. Interestingly, a common approach is to save your *'Good morning'* or *'Good afternoon'* for the adults, irrespective of any connections you have with them, but to avoid any dialogue with young people, especially if you do not know them. I would argue that this can further widen the gap and reinforce the 'us and them' mentality that isolates teachers even more when they are in the 30-versus-1 classroom situation. Reflect on how a friendly few words and an uplifting smile improves your mood yet the feeling of being blanked can send your thoughts into negative questioning as to why you were unworthy of the usual greeting. Students are no different and, even though initially they might not be expecting the informal connection with you, they are not immune to the benefits.

As I walk around my school, when I arrive in the morning and then during the day, I make a point of greeting students that I come across, whether they are on their own or in a group, and set myself a daily challenge of having at least 20 of these short *'Good morning'* conversations. Some students try to avoid my gaze and will appear uncomfortable with the interaction but, over time, the short-term boost is apparent for me and them. However, pick and choose your moments as, clearly, in some situations, such as when large groups are moving to lessons, the time taken will outweigh any benefits and you do not want to be cited as the reason for lateness: *'Honestly, Miss, I am late because Mr Singh wanted to have a good afternoon chat with me!'*

During a Year 7 residential trip, I spoke to the whole cohort about the importance of simple greetings and the mental uplift that this creates for all involved. Then one of my colleagues decided to play the practical joke of telling every room group that they had to individually wish me good morning the following day. My breakfast took a lot longer than usual!

59 Enjoy the classroom

We all enter teaching with excitement and anticipation, knowing that we will greatly enjoy being in the classroom and feel moral warmth from the difference that we will be making to the young people in our care. It is true to say that these are not the only emotions that are present, as nerves, stress and a lack of confidence can be key players too. Ask yourself which emotions you think, but more importantly which you hope, will dominate over time. Consider other adults you may meet in the world outside the alien school environment, such as supermarket checkout assistants, shop workers, tradespeople or health workers. What is the effect on you if they appear to really enjoy their job compared to those who seem to be going through the motions or act as if they are just doing you a favour? If you are disappointed

CHAPTER 5 **WALK THE WALK**

by their obvious lack of connection with their role, you probably feel sympathy for them and ask yourself why they are in that position in the first place. You might decide that they could be caught in an unfortunate situation where they are not able to do what they really want to, so have had to accept a humdrum working life.

School is no different and students will have similar thoughts running through their heads if faced with teachers who appear to loathe their job. We all can appear like this on bad days, if we are in the midst of a power struggle or wanting to show our disapproval, but this should not be the norm. In contrast, by demonstrating your enjoyment of being in the classroom, you will break down some relationship barriers and reduce the impact of the challenges that young people inevitably throw at you. What we 'look like' when enjoying the classroom will clearly differ, as we cannot all dance and glide around the room with beaming smiles, uncontrollable laughter and sweet words in a recreation of *Mary Poppins* – that would most likely result in students questioning our sanity. However, a few smiles and positive phrases can be all that is needed as you finish lessons by giving students some honest reasons why you enjoy teaching that particular group. This is especially effective when students are not expecting glowing feedback.

60 Extracurricular, extra respect

Do you remember that common question in interviews for a training place or a teaching position: *'What else you feel that you could offer the school outside of your classroom role?'* We respond and show willing by citing the numerous things that we would love to get involved in, such as trips, sports, clubs, music and drama performances or perhaps you offer to start your own extracurricular activity. These are all met by the interviewers jotting down some notes and giving you an approving smile. Fast forward into your first busy term and those thoughts are pushed back in your mind as your priority is keeping on top of your marking and planning. This you deem to be more important than helping out on some activity, even if it's an activity that students enjoy and which creates a useful opportunity to build effective relationships outside a challenging classroom. We need to strive to achieve the right balance, which will differ depending on what we teach, our subject knowledge, other responsibilities we have and, most importantly, our commitments outside school.

New teachers do need to break the cycle of spending too long planning and marking, which they may have been allowed to fall into during their training year. Allocating regular time to help with other activities should hopefully force you to become more efficient, rather than increasing the amount of time spent outside school on elements of your role that cannot be achieved during the working day. In school, it is easy to be consumed by what goes on inside your classroom, as well as by the additional duties teaching brings. However, involvement in extracurricular activities gives you a natural short-term release in a much less pressured environment and reminds you of the enjoyable learning, for students but also for you, that can take place in numerous parts of school life. In addition, slowly but surely your reputation is given a boost and naturally you gain respect which will positively impact your classroom role.

61 Aspirational pitching

Teaching a group of students with varying ability, concentration and motivation is one of the most challenging aspects of the profession but it also provides a huge psychological reward when it has been mastered, even for just a few minutes. Although the effectiveness of delivery can sometimes be difficult to judge by ourselves, there will be moments where you stand back and observe the engagement and enjoyment of learning by all the students, whatever their level.

The key question is exactly where to pitch your teaching when planning a lesson, in order to successfully navigate the choppy waters of the mixed ability river and ensure that everyone is able to make the much sought-after 'progress'. We are acutely aware of the need to support the lower end of the class, whose fragile confidence we want to build and nurture, but not in a way that belittles them or sets a low ceiling. However, boredom or a lack of challenge in learning is one of the main reasons that poor behaviour can creep into the actions of more able – and sometimes overly confident – students. Unfortunately, the classic teacher response of *'Well, if it is so easy then show me you can do it'* asks those students to enter a game that they often cannot be bothered to play.

The logical outcome might be to aim your teaching at the middle of the class and therefore minimise any issues, but I would argue that your target should be higher and you should aim for the upper quartile. This ensures that there is enough accessibility and realistic success for all. We must not forget that the large majority of students want to do well and thrive on messages that 'their level' is constantly rising, as opposed to any confirmation that their ability (and therefore outcome) is fixed.

One common strategy when setting learning activities is the 'all, most, some' approach. This can be reinforced by messages such as *'Those of you who are looking to achieve ... really need to be producing ...'* and *'None of you should accept just doing ... in the same way, you would not want anyone to tell you that you are only capable of ... and even though some might find it difficult, by pushing yourselves you definitely will improve over time'*. It is easier to encourage students to work up a level rather than ask them to slow down their pace.

62 Walk the unfamiliar school

When I started teaching, before the introduction of school-employed cover supervisors, a regular feature of the morning was the dreaded stroll to the staffroom and careful stare at the staff notice board. You looked down the list and hoped that your name would not appear to cover a lesson for an absent colleague and that you would be left with the valuable free lesson that you had already allocated to planning, marking or communicating with parents. Although I do not miss those days, I definitely feel that I gained valuable insights into aspects of the school that would otherwise be hidden from me by covering subjects such as art, drama, PE, technology or music where the classroom environments were so dissimilar to my own.

Being able to empathise with students does require knowledge of their experience, in school and beyond, so the greater your level of awareness, the better equipped you are to understand and support them more effectively. Often, as trainees or as new staff, we are required to attend a 'student shadowing day' to increase our familiarity with the school and to be able to consider what learning looks like in different settings. Yet this invaluable part of any teacher's development is often just a one-off and, as we begin our careers, we forget about most of what occurs outside our classroom or subject area. Ultimately, it is not healthy to be cooped up in one area for the whole school day, which is why the walk to a central staffroom or the lunchtime visit to the dining hall can re-energise us, before returning to our own teaching environment.

When you have a free period, take a 15-minute break to walk around areas of the school that are less familiar to you. You will not only benefit from the mental respite but will also develop as a teacher by increasing your awareness of the school in which you work – and, more importantly, the school in which your students learn.

63 Don't speak – they'll know what you're asking and thinking

When we enter teaching, a big shock to the system is the amount of talking that we do and the impact that this has on our throats and vocal chords. A common outcome is a temporary loss of our voice, usually in the first term. There are useful online guides for teachers to protect themselves against the seemingly inevitable, which mention the need to stay healthy, to speak slowly and not too loudly, and to consider pitch. We still have to accept that the increase in use of our voices when we start teaching is significant. As new teachers, we also try to hide our lack of confidence by speaking too much, overdoing explanations or filling the sound gap when there is a quiet moment in the lesson, in the same way that panic during an interview can result in poorly hidden, but thorough and repetitious, waffle. We use our voices to inform, instruct, remind, control and praise students, convincing ourselves that there is no alternative to this continual and exhausting effort.

While supporting a trainee who was overly reliant on using his voice, I set him the challenge of not talking for the first 15 minutes of a lesson. He had to carefully plan the starter so that it required zero verbal explanation and, if students were unsure, they could simply be reminded by a gesture, as the teacher pointed to the relevant area of the instructions on the board. The bemusement of the students gradually reduced and, although the target was not met, my colleague was pleasingly able to last 10 minutes without resorting to speaking. During our reflective discussion following this lesson, we were able to challenge each other on when talking is needed and when it can be replaced by actions or body language.

CHAPTER 5 **WALK THE WALK**

We also considered when teacher talk can be distracting students from messages on the board that you need them to absorb. Do you want your students to read the information or to listen to you? In addition, a key learning point was the fact that classes can be trained to develop skills such as resilience, observation and resourcefulness, so that they use other strategies instead of immediately asking the teacher when they become unsure of what to do.

You may see experienced colleagues draw a required response without words, such as when reminding students to correct their uniform or to refrain from the wrong behaviour. This two-way meeting of the minds is usually more effective than tired and predictable reminders, and the magic involved may surprise you and wow your students, taking your teaching to the next level.

64 **Play your personality**

Earlier, we discussed key principles for effective teaching: relationships, fairness, consistency, patience and challenge. Although these elements are important when we enter the profession, the blueprint of an excellent teacher can become blurry, as we need to take into account the differences in all of us. Excellent teachers can be extroverts, making use of their openly energetic and enthusiastic nature in a lively classroom situation. Yet a cautious and more reserved approach can result in equally brilliant results, as students feel protected by an element of safety in their learning. Careful planning, with the use of prescriptive resources, can be the cornerstone of great lessons for many teachers, but should not be imposed on those who thrive on spontaneity, with a greater emphasis placed on responding to cues in student responses. To suggest that only one approach can result in excellence will undoubtedly exclude those whose characteristics do not fall into that limited group.

Moreover, students value (and respond best to) honesty, not just in what their teacher says but also in how they present themselves. Young people have the gift of x-ray vision to exploit situations where teachers are losing their effectiveness as a result of being forced to adopt a style, or script, that goes against their natural approach. Trainees must be encouraged to experiment as they observe different teachers and reflect on what works best and feels most natural for them in the classroom, rather than be required to mould themselves into the image of their mentor or a 'preferred' style.

If you travel back into your own schooling, you will certainly remember, with fondness, excellent teachers who had a positive impact on you. Did they all teach in the same way? You can never be the best teacher possible unless you embrace the true 'you' – beauty, warts and all.

65 Embrace and learn from bad lessons – don't brush those experiences under the carpet

Later, as we journey into some of my biggest fails, as well as others that I have observed, it will be vital that we do not shy away from delving into the locked cupboard of our 'bad lessons'. No teacher is immune to failure through misjudging situations, making poor decisions or trying a flawed technique which, through later reflection, was obviously going to be a disaster. We are all allowed to have off days, although ideally not during an inflexible and restrictive lesson observation and school inspection process. Students, however, are usually a much more forgiving group, as long as these situations are not the norm. They often respond surprisingly well to being involved (even just as silent participants) in a reflective and honest discussion about the thought process before, during and after a teaching failure. They can be very insightful and offer feedback from a perspective that you might not have even considered.

Adopting a mindset where we place 'negatives' at the forefront of our thinking can be a challenging concept in teaching, where ultimately there is no one else to blame but ourselves and therefore apparently no escape from the prison of our inadequacies. However, accepting that you are beautifully imperfect and on a journey towards being more radiant but with fewer flaws will enable you to reach the end goal quicker and with a lighter mental load along the way. In simple terms, unless you accept your mistakes and learn from them, your development as a teacher will always be limited.

What your reflection looks like is for you to consider, as I am not suggesting that all mistakes should be followed by a public and open enquiry. Indeed, some of what you will read in the later chapter (see page 143) has been locked away deep in my brain until now. Most importantly, embrace (and even find humour in) your 'teacher fails' and know that you are not on your own. Bad lessons are happening, in secret, up and down the country, especially where teachers are new – either to the profession or to a school.

66 The great resources hoarder

One of the main reasons cited for teacher burnout or by those leaving the profession is the amount of time, outside the school day, that is taken up by the two tall pillars on which teaching adequacy rests: planning and marking. We have discussed how aspects of these can be made more manageable over time with a shift of emphasis: when marking, from teacher feedback to student learning and, when planning, aiming not for perfection but for the opportunity to teach great lessons.

However, we accept that any approach will only reduce the burden and not completely eradicate it. Creating resources can be the most time-consuming aspect of planning. Certainly, we should be encouraged to plan from scratch at times, especially when we start teaching, as often the delivery of your own ideas, which have been carefully designed and mentally walked through, will make the classroom situation easier. That said, on many occasions, there is a vast library of school and online ideas or specific resources that can be used, which will enable you to spend your limited time on small tweaks to suit your teaching style and the needs of your students. This will make teaching easier and, most importantly, the learning more effective. By asking subject leaders or colleagues *'Where are the resources for this?'*, *'What ideas are there for teaching this?'* or, much better, *'What have you used that worked well when teaching this?'*, you are not cheekily getting someone else to do your job for you. You are using the valuable experience around you to help your development. Build your bank of ideas and organise your resources so that, over a few years, you are well equipped to teach a range of topics – until of course exam specifications change and you start the whole process again! In time, advice will be sought from you and, at that point, you might reflect on the folly of new teachers being reluctant to ask for help from others.

67 Enjoy the small victories

A difficult class working quietly for a few minutes, a challenging student writing a few lines in an hour or a lesson where you did not need to give out any sanctions can all be viewed as minor positives in situations where our minds will naturally be focused on more significant aspects of our lessons. The journey from being a new teacher who is just trying to keep their head above the water and forcing a smile at the same time to the experienced and assured professional is not littered with big events but more with small changes and tweaks to both classroom practice and mental approach.

If we accept that the big picture is made up of thousands of careful and intertwined brush strokes then development as a teacher should be the result of gradual (and not necessarily linear) improvement, rather than a paint-by-numbers approach that moves from one section to the next. For example, when we have 'mastered' questioning, we can move on to 'challenge'. However, awareness of small, gradual change can be hard to detect, so we need to actively attune our focus in order to better track the progress we are making with classes, individuals or specific aspects of teaching where we are more aware of the need for improvement. In addition, by acknowledging and enjoying the small victories, we can better protect ourselves from the negativity and doubt that will wear away at our confidence, enthusiasm and ability to keep things in perspective.

68 Parents' evenings – how to manage them

The beloved annual parents' evenings … but let us stop for a moment and consider the reasoning and benefits to teachers of these intense three-hour endurance events. Clearly, it is an opportunity for you to give useful and accurate analysis of conduct and performance, with a hope that either excellence will be maintained or sustained improvements will be made where needed. Parents are given a valuable insight into a significant part of their child's life that they have limited knowledge of, due to the one-word responses ('OK', 'Good', 'Boring', 'Dunno') that children often give when their parents ask: 'How was your day?'. For students, it is either a chance to receive glowing

CHAPTER 5 WALK THE WALK

feedback, which we all welcome, to receive useful advice on how to do better, or for the dirt to be finally dished out, thus representing mental pain and torture that may result in them refusing to attend, even if the meetings are online.

The commonly held belief that students will be 'good' in the run up to their parents' evening is a myth in many cases. It will only lead to frustration for the teacher if their approach is to make comments in the classroom such as *'I am very surprised, given your parents' evening is this week, that you are behaving like that'*. This may result in students experiencing a level of anxiety but not enough for them to lose face in front of their peers when faced with not-so-subtle blackmail. Moreover, this sends the wrong message about why students should be applying themselves positively to their learning. If parent intervention is required, it should already be occurring through more regular communication.

For teachers, these evenings should not be part of a carrot and stick game but rather a chance to include parents in the learning process in a way that enhances the useful support that they can give you. When attending parents' evenings as a parent, my desire has always been to gain knowledge that can be useful to me from a teacher who clearly knows my child and is interested in their overall performance. I am looking for the teacher to provide explicit positives and negatives, rather being unable to hide their annoyance of classroom antics or, even worse, just wanting to share data with me.

The intense pace of these events can be a real challenge for new teachers, who are often the final ones left in a quiet school hall (or virtual room) late into the evening, so it is important to plan the five-minute appointments in a way that allows you to give the most important feedback, with students in a position to respond and the parents able to ask questions. This is not always easy but can be made smoother by jotting down 2 or 3 key points that you want to feed back on for each student in advance. When mastered, these evenings can feel like a cold conveyor belt process so be aware that niceties, smiles and eye contact will add an element of much-needed warmth. Where you need a brief respite or a sip of your drink, start the appointment by asking the students for their thoughts.

69 Technology – knowing when and how to use it

Interactive whiteboards, touchscreen TVs, visualisers, projectors, webcams, students with devices in the classroom, online learning platforms, quizzes that students can interact with on their phones, AI … the list of teaching technologies just seems to go on. With new facets being added regularly, it is a real challenge for anyone just to keep up. When I started teaching, I can remember easily avoiding using an overhead projector, the TV and video on wheels, or the archaic set of BBC computers that were able to run basic maths games. However, the days of having a choice about whether to incorporate technology into lessons are well and truly behind us. The vast benefits of using technology to improve student engagement, motivation and ultimately learning are obvious, and part of our role must be to teach young people how best to use it to prepare them for the world that they are going to face.

Our students need to gain familiarity with, and proficiency in, using technology outside their comfort zone of social media and gaming so that they are not disadvantaged. In addition, all schools will teach about the dangers of the online world. However, to provide balance, there is still the need for written exams to judge performance, as well as developing key learning or emotional skills that sit outside the digital universe. While some might argue that we should limit or reduce 'screen time', especially following the recent pandemic and resulting home learning, I would contend that learning with digital resources can greatly enhance excellent teaching, rather than replace it – the human still runs the show.

I am not suggesting that all our lessons need to be built around technology, but rather that we choose wisely when to introduce it. Furthermore, the effective use of engaging technology can be a useful weapon in improving behaviour, and intuitive online resources will reduce your workload when implemented appropriately. Welcoming digital aspects into your teaching does not mean ignoring the irritating potential issues, but as an excellent teacher you have back-up plans and will learn to be spontaneous and respond in the moment if the technology fails.

CHAPTER 5 **WALK THE WALK**

70 Complaints about students – keep things in perspective

Over time, we develop a wide range of useful strategies to deal with students who fail to meet our expectations for effort or behaviour. Yet these are not foolproof and we must remember the support, within school systems and through parental communication, that ultimately exists for the betterment of the young people in our care. It is not a sign of weakness or failure to refer issues to others and it is actually important for those in pastoral positions to have such information in order to better appreciate the wider picture and work with that student more effectively. Naturally, there is a level of annoyance when students seem unable to meet the basics of what you require, for example a student who never produces homework despite reminders from you and false promises from them, or whose behaviour does not improve despite your best efforts, saintly patience and flexibility to meet their needs. However, keeping such issues in perspective and not allowing ourselves to react emotionally in any written or verbal communication is a mountain that needs conquering.

It is possible that the young person in question is facing challenges that tower over any issues in your classroom and, by keeping focused on their needs, you will be able to be part of a solution rather than a victim of their actions. Consider the potential impact of a conversation with that child, where you explain the reasoning behind referring their actions to others but also demonstrate to them that you have not – and will not – give up on your role to develop and support them to succeed in your classroom. Accept that one conversation might not be enough and that persistence will gradually break down barriers. Building trust is almost always more effective than displaying disappointment.

71 Supply cover – the nightmare dream teacher job

Close your eyes and imagine a teaching role where you did not need to do any planning of lessons, any marking of work, any creation of assessments, any communication with parents or any additional administration. You are simply provided with details of what learning

CHAPTER 5 **WALK THE WALK**

tasks a class needs to do and your sole responsibility is to ensure that instructions are followed by the class. However, before you get carried away, recognise that I have just sugar coated one of the most demanding jobs in a school by highlighting the benefits that can appear insignificant in comparison to the monstrous challenges. The agency cover supervisor often sits alone in a corner of the staffroom, greeted with a *'Good morning!'* from the school's teachers, who have a blend of deep sympathy, respect and questions regarding sanity for their poor temporary colleague, knowing what the dreaded day ahead will most likely bring.

Cover supervisors enter classrooms and are met with uncontrollable excitement from students because their 'real' teacher is not in today and they have a 'cover' teacher. The excitement is not the warm and uplifting type, but it is far more mischievous in nature, as students realise there's a massive shift in the balance of power for the lesson ahead. The car crash that often follows is an example of student voice or student-directed (lack of) learning. It's not one of the controlled and focused lessons that excellent schools have running through their systems; it's more the type that happens if an army of young people are given a free rein.

Increasingly, schools have sought to employ their own cover supervisors. This gives them the advantages, over external cover staff, that come with knowing the school and quickly getting to learn about the students over a sustained period. Consider the skills that will undoubtedly be developed in these roles, where much of the teacher's time is spent dealing with low-level misbehaviour and a lack of willingness to engage in learning. I have witnessed the excellent progress of teachers who endured and survived a year of being a cover supervisor before beginning their training course. They definitely started a few steps higher than other trainees who have not had such a meaningful experience in the classroom. If you are unable to follow this path into teaching then seek to learn from cover staff in your schools by asking about the strategies they find most effective. Even better, observe them and enhance your own skills by seeking to support them, as you also reflect on your own practice.

CHAPTER 5 **WALK THE WALK**

72 **Reading, reading, reading**

With the rise of online media and information giving immediate access to knowledge, it is challenging for some young people to appreciate the benefits of actual reading. Reading can present as a long, uninteresting walk in uncomfortable conditions. When there are obvious and numerous shortcuts along the way (that seem to end at the same destination but without the exertion or poor weather), you can see why many young people would prefer to take the quick and easy option. However, it is the journey that makes you a better learner, not solely the acquisition of facts.

It is easy to find strong arguments that reading will make you '*smarter*', '*more likely to be successful*', '*improve your wellbeing*' or a '*valuable habit for anyone wanting to make their life better*', yet the importance of reading is much less advertised as students move from primary to secondary education. I am not suggesting that you introduce 'forced' reading into your lessons, as this adds to the mindset of seeing reading as a chore or imposition. Rather, share with students your experience of reading, including your enjoyment of it and the useful knowledge or thinking that you have gained as a result.

As a maths teacher, I do not feel any conflict of interest when I tell my students about never being an avid reader at school but becoming switched on and fascinated by the mental images created by reading *Richard III* and *1984* for my English GCSE. I talk to students about my love of reading about the history of maths and how that has undoubtedly made me a better teacher and, indeed, learner.

Reading can take many forms, such as novels, non-fiction books which you can dip in and out of, magazines, online articles, the news … we need to show young people that reading should be an important part of their lives and is far from boring.

Encouraging reading is not the sole responsibility of the English staff. Remember that you are a teacher of young people first and a conduit for carrying subject knowledge second.

73 The one-hour, six-lesson planning challenge

As we return to planning – one of the two tall pillars of teaching that feeds the workload monster – we hopefully appreciate that controlling the anxiety which tells us to spend hours designing a fool- (or fail-) proof lesson is a battle that we can overcome. We build confidence through reflecting on our achievements in the classroom, with a focus on effective delivery. We should cast a suspicious eye on the extent to which our thorough and detailed planning guarantees success in the unpredictable classroom, and look for ways we can increase the efficiency of our limited, precious time.

Planning a lesson in 10 minutes can initially seem daunting and perhaps you think I have set the bar too high. Working towards this achievable goal will help you to create a skeleton structure more quickly. It will enable you to focus your efforts on creativity when designing learning activities, knowing that the outline for what you want to achieve is in place. However, lessons are often not standalone in nature and learning builds from one lesson to the next, so perhaps a better approach to consider is efficient planning, for example to deliver a whole topic or unit over six lessons.

The driving force in any thinking linked to planning must be the overall learning outcomes. With this at the forefront of your mind, it is possible to work backwards from the end result to determine a path that will identify the key stepping stones along the way. List the essential areas of learning and use this as a framework from which you can link together each aspect with the next, and you will start to create a useful picture of those groups of lessons in your mind. When faced with a intimidatingly long task, we advise students to break down instructions and expectations into smaller and therefore much more manageable chunks – the idea for planning is exactly the same. Planning groups of lessons at one time will become the norm for you and can be preferable and quicker overall than planning individual sessions as a result of being immersed in the large picture of a topic rather than just concentrating on its smaller aspects.

Moreover, lessons do not always go to plan and knowing what is ahead, at our fingertips, will undoubtedly result in us being more flexible in our teaching and more responsive to the needs of our students.

74 Ensure that your classroom is an extension of you

What is the difference between a house and a home? 'House' is a coldly unemotional term referring to physical features, structural characteristics and, mainly, the outward appearance, all of which can be useful perhaps when selling a house. When we speak about our home, however, we talk warmly and lovingly about an extension of ourselves, our memories, feelings and sense of belonging. A home is where we feel safe and can thrive, whereas a house is simply where we dwell. How would you describe your classroom? In terms of your professional life, is it your house or your home?

Now let us change the viewpoint and consider what you would want your home to tell others about you when they visit. Similarly, what would you want your classroom to portray about the teacher you are? It can be easy to take the appearance of our classrooms for granted and bemoan the lack of decoration or quality of the upkeep – those are certainly not areas that fall under the responsibility of a teacher, other than to report to the appropriate colleagues. However, you can have an impact on many features of your classroom, placing the importance on the fact that it is 'your' classroom.

Taking time, or seeking support, to ensure displays reflect your passion, approach to learning or even achievements you are proud of, in addition to eye-catching student learning, will make a difference in so many areas and almost certainly have a positive impact on your practice. When you 'walk the school', inspect classrooms carefully, asking yourself these same questions. Take inspiration from the best examples even if you are *'not into'* or *'can't be bothered with'* displays. Increased pride and sense of belonging improves wellbeing. A better presented learning environment makes engagement and enjoyment more likely and messages (explicit and implicit) surrounding students can enable you to push ideas in as subtle a way as you desire. Where teachers are not privileged enough to have their own classroom castle, seek opportunities to develop some display space in the rooms you teach in – many teachers will see this as you doing them a favour.

Walk the walk key takeaways

- Teachers act as role models in all that they do: their appearance, language and character. Consider how your 'excellence' will come across to others. What are the signals that you want to be sending and what behaviours do you want your students to 'catch'? Your demonstration of patience, perspective and honestly can complement your expectation and standards incredibly well.

- You are not just a teacher in your classroom and during your lessons. Your interactions with students around the school and during extra activities can improve your reputation and thus make teaching easier. Positive communication with parents is also important – use consultation evenings to demonstrate that you have their child's best interests at heart.

- Gain from excellent colleagues in your school – how do they 'walk the walk'? Use their experience to make your teaching better and more effortless. Steal not only resources but also strategies to make planning more efficient and technology more effective in supporting learning.

- Remember that students want to learn and do well – use this when planning activities across a number of lessons. Pitch your lessons at a level that is aspirational. Explain to classes your rationale for this and they will understand that your classroom is a place where they can succeed.

- Actively support your own wellbeing by constructively reflecting on your teaching. Acknowledge your role when lessons do not go well and share your thinking with your students at appropriate times – this will increase their trust in you. Remember to enjoy the victories, however small, and use these to face challenges with positivity and the confidence that you truly are on the path to improvement.

CHAPTER 6 **TALK THE TALK**

During training programmes, how much time is dedicated to the sophisticated art of acting, including the manipulation of an audience with your voice? Are we warned that we are likely to lose our voice early in our career and should aim to speak from the chest and not the throat?

When I started my PGCE course, I quickly became aware that my ability to 'perform' in front of others was in drastic need of improvement, as it was a skill that I had never really practised or used. I had only ever used my voice for informal conversations with family or friends, to make simple requests when shopping, to make phone calls or to reluctantly respond to questions, often from those who had some sort of authority. I steered away from meeting (and lacked confidence in striking up a conversation with) anyone who I deemed to be 'new' to me. However, in the classroom, your voice is the primary weapon, with your ability to act serving as the ammunition. Although it is true to say that over time your aim improves, first you need to ensure that you are not shooting blanks or misfiring.

You 'talk the talk' to give instructions, display disappointment, hand out praise, question, build relationships, diffuse situations, increase motivation, deliver warnings and create trust – all in an effort to develop the hearts and minds of the young people in your care. Adopting simple phrases that talk about choice rather than consequence, or changing '*you*' for '*we*' when saying things like '**we don't behave like that in our classroom**', can get students on your side and diffuse tension. What we say and how we say it can turn challenging situations into manageable and positive scenarios, but getting it wrong can result in low-level issues escalating and spiralling out of our control, so choose your words carefully.

75 The controlled shout

We discussed earlier the need for empathy during tellings-off and questioned how we would like to be treated in such situations. Even though we are intelligent and logical people mostly driven by common sense, the 'teacher shout' is often released from its cage when we feel pressure, want a quick reaction or convince ourselves that we have exhausted the alternatives. However, I am not simply advocating a 'no shout' approach. We are focusing too much on the larger picture rather than seeing the finer details of what raising our voice can achieve to aid us in the classroom and, at times, when dealing with students around the school.

The key point to consider is how the shout is delivered – what we say and how we say it. A loud, uncontrolled rant informs those around us that we have temporarily lost our perspective and, although potentially scary, it serves more as entertainment for our students, who carefully observe us with a view to taking advantage of the weakness that we have laid out bare. In addition, speaking from personal experience, you can be further embarrassed when your emotions bounce around your brain, so you lose track of your thoughts. You either stop mid-sentence with a long pause, as you ponder how to continue, or you keep talking, producing what is best termed as utter nonsense.

The 'controlled shout', or just the 'raising of our voice', strengthens our position in the classroom, as we are able to project our disappointment or deliver a warning while still maintaining the assured authority without providing much of a popcorn-grabbing moment for our students. Your message should be short, to the point and specific in nature but then quickly followed by a drop in intensity and volume as your composure is retained and your feathers unruffled. A controlled *'Don't do that'* is much better than an angry *'How dare you do that'*.

76 Learn to act – watch wrestling!

Yes, you did read the line above correctly. We all bring elements of who we are into our role as teachers. I mentioned previously that I was an exceptionally shy young person and would actively avoid speaking publicly or meeting new people well into my late teens and early 20s. But teaching is an act and fundamentally we have to learn to perform on stage with confidence several times a day, learning set lines but also needing to be spontaneous in the face of pressure from a sometimes-unconvinced audience. We need to demonstrate joy, excitement, empathy, disapproval or disappointment. We need to talk effectively, even without using words, so that a smile, piercing stare, thumbs-up gesture or raised eyebrow become more important than when used with our family or friends. We have to become accomplished actors.

During a senior team planning day with the governors, we had a team-building activity where each person brought in an item that could describe them. Someone else had to consider the relevance of the item and explain that to the rest of the group. The poor governor to my right had the challenging task of explaining away my son's toy wrestling belt. After some thought, he told the room that I was into sporting competitions and keeping fit and therefore this was probably a martial arts belt from my youth. He then turned to me and asked if that was about right. I delayed my answer for as long as I could, thinking about choosing my words carefully, knowing that watching wrestling isn't necessarily considered as a refined and cultured pastime. I finally informed the room, with a smile, that the feedback was far off the mark. I went on to explain that I had been a wrestling fan since I was a child and had enjoyed sharing this with my son, who was 10 years old at the time. Most importantly, I had become increasingly aware that I had picked up so much from watching skilled wrestlers talking in a way that could thrill, amuse or anger crowds, and further build their character in a setting where delivery was always more important than the words used. I had reflected on how I spoke during assemblies, in lessons and at other times when I had to demonstrate both positive and negative emotions in a very controlled way. I explained how this had definitely been influenced by watching hours of wrestling over a number of years.

Of course, I am not saying this skill can only be picked up by watching old clips of The Rock or Stone Cold Steve Austin, but please do appreciate the need to develop your acting skills rather than lacking control and showing your real frustration, annoyance or anger. That is not effective and usually just makes you take things personally and subsequently feel worse.

77 Learn to act – watch stand-up comedy

If we explore the impact of some of the great orators of our time, whether political figures selling an idea, activists demanding a change, or actors (including wrestlers) creating an emotion, we understand that if the same words had been spoken with less vigour and adroitness, there would have been little or no change to those on the receiving end. Martin Luther King Jr, Winston Churchill, Mahatma Gandhi, John F Kennedy, Barack Obama and, more recently, Greta Thunberg all exhibit the ability to take a simple message and add honest and believable emotion, convincing the masses to march with them. However, what about a group that really does triumph or fail (or never even make it to the stage) on what they say and how they say it: stand-up comedians?

What do you call an old snowman? The joke itself is only a tiny part of the act and, as teachers, we can really learn how to manage the classroom better by watching skilled performers who create stories and images to provide context, how they lead their audience along the twists and turns of a journey and, all along the way, the audience's attention is unwavering.

CHAPTER 6 **TALK THE TALK**

We will all have our favourite comedians, from PG-friendly acts to far more risqué performers, but we should be able to capture the subtle skills of how they display confidence or vulnerability, build empathy or sympathy and maintain a level of interest in what they say. I am certainly not suggesting that we need to plan 45-minute comedy routines built around the teaching of trigonometry or plate tectonics (although that would be an interesting challenge) but rather aim to soak in the art of delivery for a clear purpose and to improve student engagement.

The answer, by the way, is water.

78 The third person in the room

Bringing wit, humour or passionate oratory skills into the classroom might go against the nature of many of us and, indeed, I was several years into my teaching before I was even close to mastering these strategies with any effectiveness. However, an easier and more mysterious simple win that seems to defy logic (and suggests a slight lack of sanity on your part) is the introduction of the invisible third person to work alongside you in leading your students. Before your eyebrows become raised and your head tilts to one side in suspicion or doubt, let me remind you that sometimes it is the small and irrational steps that result in the biggest strides forward. Students are a complicated group, bringing with them expected unpredictability but also illogical reactions to requests from you. Remember the power in asking your students to stand up instead of asking them to be quiet? Observing colleagues as part of my role has undoubtedly benefited my teaching as a result of me poaching strategies but also experiencing how different approaches can bring equally effective results.

Commonly, when I observe teachers new to the profession, I soak in energy, creativity and the bravery to take risks, yet more experienced colleagues are able to display methods that are tried and tested and appear as an extension of themselves rather than an outfit they can easily take off and replace with another. One such example was observing a science teacher with over five years of experience in my school, who often referred to herself as an enigmatic third person: 'What would Mrs P think about that answer?', 'If Mrs P wanted to design an experiment to test this, what would it look like?', 'Convince

Mrs P with that argument' or, more humorously, 'I am not so sure that Mrs P is happy with this level of noise'. Students had accepted that they had to raise their game to meet Mrs P's expectations. Trying a similar approach with younger secondary school students was natural for me in the classroom and drew positive results, with not one of them asking if I was OK or telling me that I should ask Mr S myself. It's a crazy but simple way of talking the talk and playing mind games at the same time – try it for yourself.

79 Perfect your lines

In most lessons, we probably say hundreds and hundreds of words. Although we do not carefully plan, consider and reflect on each word individually, as they flow so naturally from our tongues, we are conscious of the effect that they can have on the learning environment, both positive and negative. Over time, we fall into patterns of speech and, once habits are formed, they can stick stubbornly to us even if we are intent on replacing them with upgrades. With small tweaks, the same sentence can be delivered as an accusation, a question or a statement and therefore your intent and the resulting reaction can vary greatly. Consider these contrasting options:

- 'That was you who threw the pen.'
- 'Did you throw that pen?'
- 'Why did you throw that pen?'
- 'I am not sure who threw that pen but, whether it was you are not, I am not happy because …'

Imagine the possible reactions you could get from each comment. Of course, the actual situation needs to be taken into account, as there is a difference between catching someone red-handed as opposed to seeing the pen in question flying across the room and turning to see the prime suspect trying to contain their laughter as they meet your eye. However, if we shift our thinking to what the possible responses would be, we can be better placed to pick the line that might work best in our classrooms.

CHAPTER 6 TALK THE TALK

Even with such low-level issues, accusations can lead to instinctive denial and questions can elicit negation if only given a yes/no option, but statements might lead to a far more muted reaction, with little need or opportunity for hostility. In most situations, I would advocate an approach that leads you away from confrontation and informs your class that, while you will not be sidetracked from the importance of their learning and your teaching, you still have expectations that you will maintain and are fully prepared to up the ante when required. With more positive situations, or where praise is given, changing the emphasis from a final outcome to the effort needed along the journey will go a long way to convincing your students that you are not solely focused on the 'stars' in the class. Finish the sentence: 'Well done for …'.

Here are some phrases that I have learnt to steer away from, as well as alternatives that have worked better for me.

Instead of	Try
'If any of you do that again you're getting a detention, do you understand me?' (Leading to confrontation – if you were the student, how would you respond to this?)	'Let me remind you all about what I expect in my lessons. You're a great class so let's keep it that way, rather than having to worry about giving out sanctions. I'm way too nice to do that and you're way too nice to make me do that.'
'How dare you shout at me!' (Said in a very loud voice, demonstrating that it is OK to shout)	'There is no need for anyone to raise their voice. I'm certainly not going to shout at you. How can I help?'
'This is way too loud. You all need to work more quietly.' (Too vague)	Either: 'OK, we will have 10 minutes of working in total silence.' Or: 'We will have 10 minutes of only whispering to the person next to you, so that no one else in the room can hear.'

CHAPTER 6 **TALK THE TALK**

Instead of	Try
'Why are you talking when I am talking? That is so rude!' (Showing that you are beginning to lose your patience and giving attention to those who do not follow your rules)	'Well done to all of you who are listening. A reminder that we do not speak over others, either when one of you is answering a question or when I am talking.'
'What **does** this mean or tell us?' (Used when questioning, suggesting that there is a right answer that you are looking for)	'What **might** this mean or tell us?'

80 Only pause for applause

Have you ever experienced that oddly magical moment during a lesson where, for no apparent reason, the room becomes ghostly silent while students are completing individual tasks with only a *'you can talk to the person next to you'* rule in place? If not, I have no doubt that you will live this moment in time and then add it to your list of bizarre and irrational teaching experiences. The hypnotism does not last long, though, as a few students look around in wonder and then unfortunately one party pooper innocently (or mischievously) asks *'Why is no one talking?'*. The rest of the class instinctively share in the amazement, discuss the topic out loud and then, sadly, your mirage in the desert disappears as quickly as it materialised.

Generally, people, when in groups, will feel uncomfortable with any period of unexpected quiet and welcome any attempt to break the silence – students in a school setting are no different. This creates a potential issue in the classroom when you are in the middle of teaching and introduce a pause, either to collect your thoughts after you forget the points you needed to make, or intentionally but with little guidance for the young people on the purpose of the pause. It had taken you so long to get the class quiet in the first place and now you feel you are back at square one. When speaking to students, they can see pauses as opportunities for discussion or a break from concentrating on your

CHAPTER 6 TALK THE TALK

teaching. You need to seek to fill the gaps quickly, by repeating key points, giving praise for the quality of their focus or just talking aloud to yourself about the plans for the lesson ahead.

Two examples from my teaching career, where I know I had learnt from previous mistakes, come from outside the classroom. The first was during a school residential trip when I had to read the names for each room group, which would set even the most timid of students into a flurry of excitement. I paused throughout my long list, but I managed much better when I started by saying *'Do not talk until I have finished'* and then repeated this instruction, even when the group were already silent.

The second example comes from the exciting but dreaded end-of-year assembly where results for competitions have to be read out, a situation that students find challenging not to discuss with others around them. I took the approach of moving quickly from one set of results to the next, leaving hardly a moment to breathe. With a previous request of saving applause until the end, I was able to navigate to the end largely unscathed.

81 Explanation or argument?

Why? From the moment that children learn the basics of language, the word 'Why?' flies up the list of their favourite and most useful words when speaking to adults. Yes, those of us who are parents are all proud when our child says their first recognisable word and revel in the moment of a lovingly uttered 'Ma-ma!' or 'Da-da', even if their first word was actually 'car' or 'no'. As confidence increases, more words are introduced and simple phrases are constructed. Our joy cannot be contained until, a few years later, we desperately seek peace and quiet, with our response to the repeated question 'Why?' becoming a short and stern *'Because I said so!'*. This small, innocent word is so formidable because it has the power to prevent any discussion from ending. The ability to query responses shifts control away from the one being asked the question and the battle that ensues will usually end with the parent either losing their temper or backing down and giving in.

If we allow ourselves to fall victim to this game in the classroom then our fate will be no different. We must dissect our language to ensure that most of the 'whys' are either accounted for in what we say, to reduce the opportunity for response, or we finish by declaring, for example, *'For those of you who might be wondering why I have chosen to do this, here is my reasoning …'* However, there is no guarantee that this ruse will be effective against all students, or in all situations, so you need to prepare a statement to end any questioning that might ensue. One that I have found especially useful when being repeatedly challenged on a decision is *'Do you want an explanation or an argument? I am happy to explain but do not wish to argue with any of my students.'* In almost all cases, the response is for an explanation, not an argument (and for those who choose option B, you have already firmly shut that door) so I finish by saying *'… I accept that you might not agree and it is OK for us to see things differently, but I have explained my decision and now we must move on.'*

82 The quiet mouse

We do not always need to raise our voice to get a group of students to be quiet.

Shouting is largely considered to be an effective way of quickly getting someone's attention, alongside tapping them on the shoulder, waving your arms or even throwing an object at them – these are not all suitable in a classroom situation, though! With students, the danger is that your raised voice may subconsciously deliver a message that, if they turn up their volume, you will respond and simply talk over them, so rather than encouraging silence you are promoting the opposite. You do have the option of the 'crossed arms and stern look wait', which is akin to a game of chicken and its success is reliant on the relationship that you have built with the group. Perhaps a more effective method is praising those students who have settled down and are ready to learn, hoping that others will decide that they would rather be a part of those to whom you are directing your attention. As with any simple win, you are best placed to choose the most appropriate response, given the needs in your classroom.

However, do experiment by introducing the 'quiet mouse' into your lessons, in situations where you need calm and focus from your students. By lowering your voice so that is barely audible, you are presenting yourself as slightly vulnerable but still in total control.

CHAPTER 6 **TALK THE TALK**

Students are left with two choices – either they continue talking, knowing the element of rudeness in this option, or switch their focus to trying to work out the importance of what you are saying, as well as why you are talking so quietly. Is this not another game of chicken? Well, yes, and if any doubts stem from thinking that the noise will be so high that no one will hear you anyway then accept that some students, even one or two, will spot what is going on. Then you can get ready to be surprised by the power of that little mouse. You can raise your voice if needed, but keep it fairly quiet to ensure that students need to work harder to concentrate on what you are saying, at the detriment of their previous noisy activities. The mouse does need its rest, though, and overuse will lessen its powers.

83 Buying yourself time

As an avid sports fan, I have been known, from time to time, to shout at my television when a referee seems to lack any ounce of common sense and makes a decision that, from the comfort of my living room and with access to replays, I can easily see was not correct. In addition, the introduction of video technology both reduced and highlighted the number of key errors, although frustration (which is probably a deviant form of enjoyment) still exists and not every small incident can be reviewed.

However, having experienced the role of a referee or linesperson myself, I do appreciate the impossible challenge of being able to spot everything and to always make the correct call in a matter of seconds. Many of the snapshot decisions we make in the classroom are not too challenging in nature and the stakes are relatively insignificant, so errors can be swept under the carpet with little need for explanation. Bigger incidents, though, are not so easy to judge or react to in the moment and have a greater need for a measured, calm and appropriate response. Yet we feel the pressure, from onlooking students, of immediately taking charge and demonstrating that certain behaviours are totally unacceptable and cannot be allowed to go unchecked. You do not have the advantage of video replays and are often not in a position to consult with other adults who can act as witnesses, so you need to create time and thinking space for yourself while still maintaining your assured authority. Sending students to wait for you outside the classroom can enable you to display your feelings of disappointment but also negate the need for immediate action. Alternatively, you can instruct the class to continue with their learning activities, assuring them that the incident will be dealt with but highlighting the need for calm for all parties. You could even request a (good or innocent) student to call for a nearby teacher or senior member of staff. The incident itself will largely dictate the best course of action, as the responses required for a classroom fight or extreme behaviour between students will differ for defiant or aggressive behaviour that is directed mainly towards you.

84 The ineffective angry teacher – remember the dream?

Do you remember the classic teacher nightmare that disturbs our peaceful sleep in the few days before a school return? We will probably all share a similar mental image of a group of students refusing to follow any of our instructions, which then become unmet demands with a stark realisation of our utter ineffectiveness and, as a result, our anger quickly bubbles up to the top of our glass. Thankfully we wake up just before it can overflow. These episodes live in our subconscious, hidden away in a dark, locked room that we visit less and less as we progress with our teaching.

But rather than discard the dream as the unhelpful creation of a tired and overactive mind, there may be value in deciphering the camouflaged messages and aiming to unlock the wisdom that resides in this dark tale. We wake up in a cold sweat, not because our actions are veering towards a distinct lack of professionalism and therefore possible dismissal from our role, but because the image we saw does not in any way look or behave like us. We do not recognise the negativity, annoyance and anger, yet we should accept that being frustrated in the classroom is a sign that we care and therefore is a natural response in the face of a challenging group.

Such classes do take time to turn, and this is often more a case of months than days or weeks, so patience has to be the key. Patience, however, does not mean accepting poor standards or being a walkover. It refers more to mental resilience and unfaltering persistence from one lesson to the next. Calmly and logically, talk to the class about your disappointment but also (and more importantly) your absolute belief that they are a good group and they will realise that themselves in time with your teaching and support. Do this at the end of a lesson, at the start of the following one or at any point where their focus makes it possible.

Informing a group of young people that you will not give up on them is a powerful message, especially in cases where they have had to endure a lack of consistency with several changes to their teacher, sometimes within the same term.

85 Breaking the silence

As discussed earlier, any gaps or pauses in your verbal information to a class, or the randomness of a brief moment of quiet, can open the floodgates and encourage students to fill the void. Yet there will be silent moments in lessons by your design. Silence can be unnerving but, in the classroom, it represents peace and tranquillity, and the ideal environment for when complete concentration is required. Being able to achieve and then sustain silence when students are doing individual learning tasks is no mean feat. I would argue that all new teachers need to experiment with ways of accomplishing this outcome, so that they can gain confidence from knowing that this strategy is safely in their locker, to use if and when they need it.

Depending on the situation and nature of a group, managing periods of quiet that are longer than about 10 minutes represents a true challenge, but not one that is insurmountable if **you** take on the role of the silence breaker at the point where you can sense the changing of the tide. Deploying a calm, quiet, hypnotic voice to give important reminders about their learning, as well as to praise their effort, can squeeze out a few more minutes of silence and, more importantly, give a smoother transition to the next activity. Providing a countdown of time remaining, at certain points, can be effective in getting close to the full allocated period for silence. This can be done with a visible counter but do be aware that these are too honest and lack flexibility. For example, I will often tell students that they have five minutes left and then, after observing positive engagement, five minutes later I tell them that they have two or three minutes to go.

In addition to skilfully breaking the silence at the end of a period of calm learning, peace can be attained at a much earlier stage by dealing with student questions quietly and at their desk. Responding in public would encourage more questions in a seemingly open forum and undoubtedly disrupt the serenity in the classroom.

And, of course, if all else fails, there is always the reliable '*Shhhhh!*', starting at a higher volume and then lowering the level gradually.

86 Tweaking your (high) expectations

'The next person who speaks, or steps out of line, will be getting a detention – do you understand?'. This collection of words is one of the most basic of all classroom threats, born out of frustration and the emptying of the patience cup but it leaves us with few other options. The entertainment that ensues tests the limits of the ultimatum and loses the genuine questions, such as requests for help with the learning, or to leave for a music lesson or to point out an error in our board work. And what about the students who are more roguish in nature?

Also, reflect on the complaints from students who were given a punishment for just 'coughing' – we know that the real situation was not so simple but we could have prevented our teaching approach from being brought into question. Perhaps this is a mistake that many of us have made in the classroom and then quickly realised how our reactive comment has put us in quite a tricky position. However, it is not too late to make a few subtle changes to our communication by adding an element of measured thinking and sharing a clearer definition of '*stepping out of line*'.

Getting the right balance between expectations that are unrealistic and those that are aspirational but achievable will be largely mastered over time, as we become more familiar with our classes. Yet, even where a situation has been misjudged, we can, after careful observation and consideration, make small modifications to lower the high bar we have set to a more acceptable level. This is almost always easier than working up from an unambitious starting point and then, after the class have bought wholeheartedly into your casual approach, trying to convince them that you expect more. In addition, there are

CHAPTER 6 **TALK THE TALK**

times when your demands can be too specific and you are better off adding an element of vagueness to your stated expectations. Consider the differences between *'You are not allowed to talk'*, *'There should be no talking'*, *'I should not be able to hear you'* and *'You should all be working quietly'*. All of these instructions can be tweaked, but some of the comments require a bigger compromise, leaving your shift in expectations more obvious.

87 Build up to negatives and positives

'I'm afraid I have some bad news for you'. Then comes the long pause, with a rapid switching of camera angles paired with tense music akin to a pounding heartbeat. Finally: *'You've made it to the next round!'* Cue shrieks, screams, applause, uplifting sounds and a mischievous smile on the judges' faces.

I am not suggesting that your classroom becomes the *X-Factor* studio or that you put any of your students through a mini emotional rollercoaster for the pleasure of the others, but we can certainly take advantage of the skill in building up to comments, to place greater emphasis on the message that we want to share, positive or negative. We want our students not only to fully appreciate our words in the moment, but most importantly to remember them and therefore be able to act on our advice when the lesson is long over. This could be a big ask for some students, as we know how quickly our brains forget information, but we also know how sticky some words can be if they have increased substance, relevance or intrigue.

'I am disappointed because …', is clear and concise and can be easily launched by our vocal chords, yet they enter a student's brain and then leave without even touching the sides. However, building up to the significance of your comments with anecdotes, reflections or questions for the students to ponder, and with maybe no obvious signs of where this train of thought might be heading, can keep the door of attention open for longer rather than it being shut immediately in the face of more obvious criticism.

With a similar mindset, giving out praise can last a few seconds (and for individual positive feedback this might be more welcomed) or it could form part of a more meaningful episode in the highly important motivation and development of your students. Are you now wondering how much of your precious lesson time might be taken up by these stories, to the detriment of your teaching? Firstly, I would not see this as a feature of every lesson and, secondly, think about your priorities as a teacher and where improving your students' character sits among the other things that you are trying to achieve.

88 Distracting the negatives

Think about how you would deal with a friend who seeks your support with an issue that has made them feel anxious, unhappy or plain angry. You could demonstrate that you entirely share their frustration and thus legitimise their emotions. Depending on your friend, this could give them helpful reassurance or it could backfire, bringing more of their negativity to the surface and intensifying their feelings. Demonstrating understanding and showing moral support can, however, be done in a way that also lays out a path to improve their mood. The friend might want a distraction rather than go through the fine details of their grievance. Much will depend on the situation itself and the relationship between the two of you, but it might also be helpful to consider the type of support that would most help **you** if the roles were reversed and you needed the ear of a partner or a friend after a tough day?

An aspect of the unpredictability of teaching is sometimes being faced with negative or unhappy students at the start of your lesson. It is not because of anything that has occurred since they set foot in your domain, but it's due to factors unrelated to their relationship with you, such as issues with a teacher from a previous lesson, a falling out between peers or challenges they are facing in their home life. If you ignore or trivialise their emotions, then the student concerned will remain downbeat and not fully engage with your teaching. However, if you allow them a forum to present their case in public then not only might there be resulting issues for you from a professional or safeguarding angle, but also the opportunities for others to comment will simply make things worse.

You need to work towards achieving a better balance. By acknowledging the student's feelings, you do not need to enter into any discussion but can show a degree of empathy. You can give advice to preoccupy themselves with your lesson – *'I can see that you are* down or not yourself and if you need to speak to me later then you can. When I feel in a similar way, it helps for me to …. How about I start the lesson and see how we get on?'. You may only have a minimal effect on their mood, but everyone can benefit from even a small improvement. Remember that feeling positive (or indeed negative) is infectious and which of those feelings would you like to spread?

89 Cold comebacks

Humour can take many forms, such as physical, self-deprecating, surreal, improvisational, dry wit, dark, slapstick and observational. While I would advise you to steer away from certain types of humour in the classroom, there is much to be gained by carefully introducing amusing moments into your lessons. In addition, excellent teachers develop an ability to deflect negativity and can effectively de-escalate situations through short, light-hearted responses that do not alter the flow of learning. However, until students have personally witnessed the mastering of this art, they can still seek to challenge their teacher with questions, comments or responses that are designed to investigate the limits of patience and the strength of resolve. I learnt quickly that, when being tested by students, long public discussions or the need for thorough justification of my decisions had little benefit in the classroom and largely ended with me taking the role of a puppet whose strings were being pulled by my (not so) innocent students.

I therefore sought to learn the art of lukewarm comebacks that walked the fine line between demonstrating too much care or empathy and the dangerous, unwelcome sarcasm which indicates a lack of real interest on your part. I certainly made my mistakes on the way, taking time to find the correct temperature. Responding to a challenge with phrases like *'Erm, no, I don't think so'*, *'That is really interesting, but no'* or *'Good point, I shall have to remember that, thank you. OK, let's move on'* does have to be delicately managed as I am sure you can envisage such comments backfiring in the wrong situation or with the wrong class. With careful refining (and by adding meaningful eye contact with a genuine smile), you will be able to form a habit of not entering into unhelpful dialogue when being challenged. Importantly, as we talk the talk, remember it is not just what you say, but how you say it.

Talk the talk key takeaways

- Our voice is the primary weapon in the classroom and is key to defining high standards, setting the tone for a focused learning environment and dealing with incidents. Therefore, we must carefully consider both what we say and how we say it. Accept that speaking confidently and convincingly in front of others is an art form which needs to be developed and practised.

- We can learn from others who use their voice to motivate, elicit emotional reactions and entertain their audience, such as actors, comedians and public figures. Absorb ways in which varying the volume of your speaking, from the controlled shout to the barely audible, can be effective in dealing with different types of classroom situations.

- Develop your go-to lines when dealing with low-level issues, to avoid confrontation and de-escalate situations at the same time as demonstrating your authority and composure. You can deliver positive or negative feedback in a number of ways to have greater impact, given the situation and those on the receiving end.

- Silence is golden but can quickly be broken. Consider how your planning and delivery can create and extend periods of quiet learning by pre-empting where gaps might occur and by responding to student questions individually and discreetly. Manage pauses in your teaching carefully by using reminders or praise.

- New teachers might overly rely on their voice and the parts of the lesson where they are talking to a class can be too long, leading to a lack of focus and engagement. Your non-negotiable is silence when you are speaking, but it is almost impossible for anyone to concentrate for extended periods. The right balance will differ from one group to another. If you need help, refer to the 'mysterious' third person!

CHAPTER 7 **MIND GAMES**

Santa Claus, the Tooth Fairy and Halloween. As children, we are encouraged to believe in the impossible. Our eyes are opened with wonder and amazement as we learn about the special cases that live outside the clearly defined borders of the 'real world', in a realm where harmless mystery roams free. Our innocence is manipulated as a belief system is erected in our minds in order to shape our behaviour, but also to provide us with joy and hope. Even when our innocence departs and the worldwide con is slowly revealed, we embrace these magical experiences not as lies but as treasures of our childhood, without which our imagination, creativity and potential would be limited.

Sawing a person in half and then instantly reconfiguring their body behind a simple-looking curtain will no longer pierce through our rational protective screen but we do accept the artistic and entertainment value of the performance. If we compare tales of the impossible with those that stretch human boundaries, our absolute attention to the act is evidence of the power of suggestion to hypnotise and control an audience. We have already established the performance element of the excellent teacher who can introduce wonder and amazement to make their classroom presence more mesmerising, but there are simple tricks that all teachers can perfect to enhance their aura. These are not dark arts but strategies to make learning more enjoyable, authentic and helpfully unpredictable.

90 Tales of the unexpected

What was the last film you watched that caught you on the back foot, as an unexpected twist in the plot pulled you deeper and deeper into the experience? *The Sixth Sense, Shutter Island, Predestination, Talaash* and *Parasite* are some of my favourites. They all directed my thinking one way and then forced my mind into a sharp turn. As I was slowly trying to reconfigure my bearings, I gripped on tightly and revelled in the slow train ride that ended as a thrilling roller coaster. Even those with greater wisdom, who can see the bumps in the road well in advance, have to accept the enjoyment which can be derived from not being able to completely picture the journey ahead. Predictability can provide much-needed reassurance and safety in the classroom, but if the story of a lesson is clear from the start, where is the excitement or discovery in the learning? In addition, the long, straight road with clear skies and repetitious scenery is less likely to reside in our long-term memory than a route that is laden with mild peril, such as the thunderstorm as we travel through a dense jungle.

Experiment with the unknown at the start of a lesson, by raising a question which has no obvious answer and teasing possible routes that students could explore – but also warn them of the dangers along the way, with the reassurance that you will be their passenger, as silent or vocal as needed. We are, of course, talking about dangers of confusion, misinformation or contradiction.

Alternatively, set up your 'safe' lesson with clearly defined outcomes but, just as the end is in sight, ask students to sift through their memory of your teaching in the past hour and question you to try to unearth the two or three errors that you subtly dropped along the way. As you build your skills, identify the most amenable class and introduce them into the planning conversation for future learning. Take advantage of their creativity in order to develop their character and robustness to be able to cope outside their comfort zone with greater confidence.

I must end with the obvious word of caution about not overusing the plot twist, as unpredictability can become tedious and lack entertainment value with greater exposure and familiarity, if used too often.

91 The line between confidence and arrogance

As actors who perform multiple times every day, five days a week and nearly 40 weeks a year, we are required to perfect a multitude of emotions to enhance our credibility and gain the trust of our students, who need to fully believe in our portrayal of enjoyment, disappointment, pride, vulnerability, empathy, anger or bemusement. However, we are not just there to provide an hour of entertainment. Our main roles are to educate and nurture so that our audience has confidence and trust in being in our care – the burden is not insignificant. Outside the world of education, the demands placed on teachers are akin to those that a manager of numerous employees may experience where they are expected to see all, know all and do all, smiling and showing true humanity along the way with no room for errors or emotive reactions. The elevated position of the one in control who holds power over others can mutate their confidence into arrogance with an overfeeding of a previously silent ego.

The most effective leaders are considered to exude confidence (and as a result gain respect from their colleagues) but also demonstrate humility and sit inside their team rather than outside or above it. Being an effective teacher is no different. For some, like me when I started teaching, it might be a challenge to display high levels of confidence but this does need to be developed in order to gain the trust of your students and firmly place you as the leader in the classroom. However, an inability to rein in your self-belief can lead you down the path of becoming the arrogant teacher that students might fear and not question. They will never fully buy into, or catch from you, the positive qualities that are increasingly hidden from them. Finding the right balance will take time but the pot of gold at the end of the rainbow will gift you the ultimate teacher skill: to inspire and be a role model to your students.

92 Sweet little lies

The first car I ever bought was a royal blue Ford Fiesta. It was second hand, had done only about 15,000 miles and, most importantly, had one very careful previous owner who only made short journeys of no more than a few miles – a vicar in his 60s. I wonder where this vast army of older church folk, who purchase new cars and after a few years pass them onto car dealers unscathed, reside and whether they are paid to offer this valuable service to the community to ensure that first-time drivers have such good deals. Maybe I was misled and instead the previous owner was not such a reliable and respectable person – I wonder whether the price would have remained the same with this different story. Although we can all perch on those elevated four-legged creatures (sitting on your high horse), we should not completely discount the skills of car salespeople who give stretching the truth a whole new meaning. Sometimes, we do need protecting from the truth or being shown that, to move forward, there are more important things than factual rights and wrongs.

In the classroom, if we always shared our true feelings or 'said it how it was' then our career might be short lived or at least be a rocky ride, so we must accept that there will be an element of lying to our students in order to protect, support or preserve. I am not referring to the huge whoppers that lack credibility, as we also recognise our duty to guide our young people both from a moral and ethical standpoint, but, rather, more subtle statements that will steer away from any dispute or controversy.

CHAPTER 7 **MIND GAMES**

I use a simple example of this by rewarding a class for their excellent effort with no compulsory homework – when I was not planning to set any anyway: *'I am so impressed with your effort and attitude to your learning today. As a result, we have made much better progress than I had hoped and I do not need to set you any homework.'* Note that I spoke about homework rather than home learning to draw out the bonus in their reward. Alternatively, when reprimanding or sanctioning a student, you could mention how you have been extra kind about the level of punishment due to your firm belief in their character and willingness to improve, when you had already settled on the outcome and decided their punishment. If such thoughts leave you aghast, think about the twisting of facts that may occur in an appraisal meeting or, even better, your last interview or your response to your child's first drawing – *'That is so good! You are a great artist!'*.

93 Use the force

If we simplify the behaviour management aspect of teaching to one basic premise, I would argue that it is the challenge of persuading your students to do exactly what you want them to do. This is no mean feat when dealing with 30 increasingly independent young people, many of whom have a natural inclination to test both the solidity of the boundaries presented to them and the strength of your resolve in maintaining them. Raising your voice may result in a short-term fix but the spirit of defiance keeps growing steadily, as the root of the issue has not been addressed and your controlled anger becomes less effective with increased use. In contrast, being quiet and firm can be successful most of the time but the delivery of a subtle rebuke has to be carefully considered from the perspective of students, so that it does not share the same fate as the teacher shout. Any *Star Wars* fan will remember the intrigue of learning about the 'force' and marvelling at the simplicity of seeing it in action. Obi-Wan Kenobi's line *'You don't need to see his identification – these aren't the droids you're looking for'* is repeated back by a faceless Stormtrooper – Kenobi has accomplished a classic manipulation of the mind.

Is there a place for the 'force' in your classroom, without the need for you to wear a long robe and carry a toy lightsabre? Any bid to encourage another person to act in a particular manner can be

CHAPTER 7 **MIND GAMES**

presented in a variety of ways, ranging from a short, direct instruction to a softer, convincing request. Your Jedi powers can be introduced with words that require a particular response or by informing the receiver of what they want and what they do not want. We have previously discussed ending an order with *'Thank you'* and walking away with an expectation of the desired outcome, but you can also be persuasive by, for example, turning *'Please don't do that'* or *'Stop doing that'* into *'You don't want to do that (now)'* or *'We don't do that in here'*. I cannot promise that you will get your words repeated back to you in a zombie-like fashion but subtly changing your tone from a statement or demand to an empathetic and inclusive piece of advice may achieve results that surprise you.

94 Talk choices

A lack of responsibility can result in the loss of influence over your destiny but it can also come with a welcome lack of culpability and freedom from criticism. Even for the most adamant of control freaks, this can be appealing from time to time. Consider the students in your domain. You are clearly the one in charge (and hopefully control), with them simply responding to your instructions and being carried along in the direction you have set. Therefore, whenever issues arise, they can absolve themselves from any accountability and apportion blame to you and your teaching, to the classroom environment, to each other or to their own brain that *'did not think'*. However, we know that they are not so innocent. From the outset, we should all seek to develop our students to become successful learners but also and more so, better people. To achieve this, they need to take ownership. They need to be reminded that their actions are mostly deliberate and are a direct result of their own thoughts and desires, rather than purely impulsive responses to changes in their surroundings.

When I was faced with a particularly challenging group who, repeatedly and en masse, broke through my attempts to manage them, I took a risk and decided to appeal to their better nature not with pleas or bribery, but by appearing to hand over the reins of power – an incredibly scary thought! With the support (and in the presence) of a senior member of staff, I spoke individually to the four most disruptive students about the choices that they were making and the impact that was having on me. As a mathematician, I am a fan of using

CHAPTER 7 / MIND GAMES

a simple structure when trying to make a point. I told each student that in my lessons they had three distinct choices and asked them to reflect upon which choice they had deliberately been opting for:

- Number 1: they could choose to make it easier for me to teach the lesson by behaving well, responding to my questions and working hard.

- Number 2: they could have no real impact on my ability to teach by being passive and quiet, and going through the motions, doing just enough to get by.

- Number 3: they could make it harder for me to teach by being disruptive, rude and defiant.

Each student accepted that they had chosen number 3, but were pleased that I did not blame or criticise them as a young person and just accepted that these were bad habits that they had fallen into. Talking about choices gave them control but also responsibility. They certainly did not transform into angels but my relationship with them did improve and there was a shift more often from option three to two.

95 Magic and mystery

'This guy is a human calculator – he can do trig in his head!'. This was part of a review about me on the now-defunct ratemyteacher.com, where anyone, not always students, could post an anonymous review and 'rate' their teacher. (Yes, you are right, it was an absolute recipe for disaster and a horrible platform for abuse.) As we return to the performance aspect of classroom teaching, we should consider the impact of adding a few subtle drops of mystery into our persona and introducing an element of unfathomable skill into our weaponry. We might have impressive talents that have taken years to perfect, such as the ability to juggle while delivering an assembly, solving a Rubik's Cube in seconds or having a photographic memory when it comes to capital cities of the world. However, I am referring more to the art of deception to suggest that you can, for example, read minds or predict the future, without ever standing in front of your class and claiming to be able to do so – otherwise, you will be put to the test and your failure will shatter the short-lived illusion.

You might be disappointed to hear that I cannot do trigonometry in my head, but I can plan to do a particular question that requires finding a value, which can be remembered a few seconds before working through it in a lesson. *'OK, so we have the hypotenuse and have to calculate the adjacent, so we need to do 15 times cos(38). Erm, let me think, cos(38), cos(38) – er, I think that is about 0.788. Is that right? You will obviously need to use your calculators. It is? Great, so now we can finish the question'*. The challenge to keep a straight face when looking directly at your students displaying bemusement or shock, as they clean their glasses or retype the value into their calculator to double check, is one that must be overcome as you continue with the lesson as normal. Why would someone who **can** do 'trig in their head' stop to marvel at such an expected occurrence? After all these years, my secret is out.

If you cannot think about how such mystery could be introduced into other subject areas, try, when monitoring and supporting your class while they are working, to remember a few words that some students have written and use this in your feedback without referring to anyone in particular: *'Some of you might have thought about … when considering the key factors of female emancipation …, did anyone? Ah, a few of you did. Well done, you have shown that you can associate … with …'*. You are not claiming to be able to read minds, in the same way that I never awarded myself human calculator status, but you are drawing attention towards key learning and away from the many classroom distractions that will sideline your best intentions.

96 Develop their memory, build their confidence

'Demonstrating impact' is a term that I sometimes view with suspicion while having to justify how effective a strategy has been, when quantitative data can be largely a work of fiction. With an increasing element of research and development in schools, as well as accountability to those who monitor and assess you, we enter the game of linking actions to outcomes in a multidimensional situation. However, achieving success is a feel-good moment that we all want to experience in all we do and is the best reward for our hard work. Our students are no different and, by creating situations in lessons that

CHAPTER 7 **MIND GAMES**

produce tangible 'impact', you can increase their positivity as well as their faith, and therefore respect in your ability to make them succeed if they succumb and follow your guidance.

The balance between knowledge and skills exists in all subjects. Being able to correctly remember facts in order to effectively apply them can be considered as the ongoing game in learning – without one piece in the right place, the position of the other becomes pretty much irrelevant. Simply put, your students need to be able to recall information. We can introduce memory palaces or turn to learning by rote, yet do we need moments in lessons where students can practise and then be assessed in low-pressure situations with achievable success. You may need to start with the obvious facts to demonstrate that they have (and can) retain information. This will not only increase their self-belief but will also make them more determined as you increase the range of what needs to be memorised.

When preparing for (or reviewing) tests, talk to your classes about where memory was needed to be able to access a question and where the application was needed in order to answer it. This might need to be a common feature of exam classes where momentum and confidence are paramount. Finish these activities with a simple discussion in which you explicitly draw out the impact of their efforts. Show them that your classroom is a place where the believers succeed and those who are yet to succeed can clearly understand the 'what and how' of their next steps. Everyone likes the taste of an achievement that is truly earned and, although some students may be slower to convert, you will have done your job of clearing the path for them. Demonstrating your impact on their improvement in a basic area such as memory is a simple win that will have knock-on effects for the more challenging parts of teaching.

97 Be larger than life

I have often thought about writing a comedy sketch show where I could share the vast amounts of humour, joy and unpredictability, the highs and the lows, that make up a teacher's life with the public, whose own experience of being in the classroom is hidden away, eroded by the sands of time or masked by seeing education from a parent's perspective rather than a child's one. Maybe this would serve as a better recruitment drive than the current Disneyesque adverts. One moment that I would love to recreate is where a teacher delivers an Oscar-worthy performance, a truly inspirational monologue displaying a clear love for the subject and finishes by asking if there are any questions, almost expecting a round of applause with flowers being thrown from the audience. The camera then pans to the students, who are either looking out of the window, hitting each other with rulers or trying to sneak a moment on their phones. The deflation of the teacher is evident. However, a moment of hope is introduced when an angelic-looking child raises their hand and the teacher excitedly asks what the question is, hoping that this will transform their lesson as it hangs precariously to the cliffside. What aspect of the teaching did the child want to explore further? Among the classroom chaos, has the teacher planted a seed of passion in this student that will stay with them for their whole life? After a lengthy pause and the rest of the class looking on, the question is asked: *'Excuse me, Miss, can I go to the toilet please?'*. Deflation, hope, deflation.

Contrast this with the special breed of educators that we all remember, possibly with fondness or possibly with suspicion – the skilled eccentric teacher who resides in their own bubble which offers protection from the challenges of the classroom as they march on, seeming oblivious to overt ridicule or subtle mocking. I would argue that this created persona, suggesting a lack of a normal level of awareness of surroundings and of others, is truly an act of genius. Reflect on how often these teachers managed to control classes – was it mainly because the students, having unleashed their attacks with no success, decided to fall in line, not even sure of why themselves but mentally exhausted as they try to make sense of the unfathomable.

CHAPTER 7 **MIND GAMES**

I am not suggesting that turning yourself into a crazed, unhinged person is either desirable or a simple win, but introducing an element of complexity into the 'teacher you' can have surprisingly positive results when more logical methods have failed. Not being afraid to talk about the true passion you have for teaching and your subject, changing course in a lesson just because you want to, or talking (seemingly) off topic leads your students away from being able to predict your next move, if it happens sparingly, spontaneously and, of course, convincingly. Consider lines like this:

- *'That is such an interesting response to my question, amazing. I think I am just going to ponder on that for a minute. So, so interesting.'* Or:

- *'... having learnt about springs, let's just all think about the beauty in learning physics, which cleverly describes the world around us, absolutely crazy but in a good way.'* Or even:

- *'I wish this lesson was two hours long so we could truly explore this character, learning how and why he was doomed from the start. I know that we all will find this so, so fascinating'.*

98 **Eyes-closed feedback**

Having a clear understanding of what students experience in lessons is crucial to becoming an excellent teacher. However, when I use the term 'experience' I am not referring to the functional aspects of being a learner, I am asking you to reflect on the emotions, feelings and pressures that exist for a young person in the classroom, where perceptions of other students are often far more important than how the teacher views them. We speak to our students about not being afraid to answer questions, ask for help or contribute to class discussions – but how do **we** respond when the same is required from us? Despite trying to create a culture in my classroom where all students feel 'safe' to speak up, I am aware, from my own experience, of how huge an obstacle this can be for some. Actually, in professional development sessions with other teachers I am equally guilty of keeping quiet, even sometimes when I believe that I have an interesting and valid point to make. For me, hands-down questioning (or 'cold calling') has helped to reduce students' fear of speaking

CHAPTER 7 **MIND GAMES**

in front of the class, but obviously this does require knowing how to respond to incorrect or irrelevant points, in order not to shatter anyone's confidence, as well as a knowledge of your class so that asking students 'randomly' is more of a calculated process than is being suggested.

However, questioning can be a prolonged process with contributions from only a few. There are other methods to gain feedback from the whole class, such as using mini whiteboards, traffic light cards or thumbs being up, to the side or down. I sometimes find these methods flawed when many in the class are unsure of an answer and the game that ensues involves students looking at each other (or, more often, just at the 'bright kid') to gauge what the right answer is. Getting responses in multichoice situations (or when you want yes, no, don't know feedback) without students being influenced by each other can seem challenging unless you have 30 soundproof booths in your classroom. I spent years battling with this until I saw another teacher ask their class to close their eyes and then put their hand up, at the right time, to answer A, B or C. It is true that classes will need training for this to work but actually I found that it was not as difficult as I had expected. The beauty of this method is that students can answer without fear of ridicule if they have gone for the obvious wrong answer, but also as a teacher I can alleviate any disappointment by tweaking the numbers. If, for example, only one student went for B, one went for C and the rest opted for the correct answer A, I can respond by suggesting that 'many' got the right answer and 'some' went for B and C, explaining what the thinking should be to arrive at the correct conclusion and why some might have opted for the incorrect answers. You can still ask an A student to explain the rationale behind their choice and (if you want) ask a B or C student to reflect on their misconceptions in order to help them understand and improve. For me, this is a simple win that is a fairly common feature of my lessons now, across all age groups.

CHAPTER 7 **MIND GAMES**

99 A routine that students love

Lining up in silence outside the classroom before the lesson starts, standing behind chairs and quietly waiting for the teacher to ask you to be seated or a focused start where learning objectives are explained. As the lesson progresses, having elements of listening to the teacher, whole-class discussion where students learn from each other, quiet activities and a chance to work collaboratively. The end of the lesson consisting of a review of learning, packing away sensibly and then dismissing the class in silence, row by row, with a mutual '*thank you*' as they depart.

I have just described a basic plan for an orchestrated and well-managed lesson which should not come as a surprise to you – yet we know in practice that it is not so easily achieved, as we are faced with complex young people who (thankfully) do not operate robotically.

Even though I highlighted earlier the dangers of lessons being too predictable, and as a result possibly mundane, routine is the teacher's best friend, who sits quietly, watching in the corner, ready to intervene if and when there is a need for structure and order. Moreover, I firmly believe that students value knowing how a lesson will usually play out. This provides a welcome, safe environment which may sometimes contrast with their experiences outside the classroom, as well as their feelings and emotions which are a thrilling but scary ride during their teenage years.

To help students embrace routine, give them ownership over its design and reasoning. This mind game is not an example of deception, even though you have the final say and clearly will only adopt a suggested model which creates a purposeful learning environment. It develops your students by shifting their position in your classroom from passive passengers to helpful back-seat drivers giving directions and words of encouragement so that you do not zone out while at the wheel and miss a crucial turning. Through this shared decision making, allocate time, as required, to reflect on the effectiveness of 'their' routine. Look to make refinements where improvements can be made – ensuring that your class understands the rationale, not as a punitive measure but as a positive change. Try this with an upcoming topic where your plan is not fully decided.

100 Student-led learning

The term 'student-led learning' is often misunderstood. To suggest that we hand over the reins and let our students dictate the content and design of lessons will send cold chills down the spine of many a teacher; the phrase *'letting the inmates run the asylum'* springs to mind. Having sought feedback on numerous occasions from my classes on what they thought would make learning more enjoyable and effective, I am aware of the dangers of asking such open questions. Some will respond honestly – especially the more vocal and challenging students as opposed to the quiet, engaged and quietly successful ones – and from one perspective: more videos, more trips, less writing and being allowed to choose who they work with in groups. What could possibly go wrong? And, in fact, why did I not think of those wonderful ideas myself?

However, the idea of meaningfully including your students when drawing up the blueprint of learning activities (and therefore sharing in its success or failure) is entirely reasonable and gives the most important collective in the classroom ownership, responsibility and accountability. As part of their wider development, groups should be supported by being made aware of the learning goals, given examples of potential options for activities and helped to identify key objectives to assess how well their aims were met. Your role in leading the learning remains unchanged but you elevate your students, resulting in them sitting at the same table, with you at the head, of course. This is likely to improve their behaviour.

With many simple wins, the key is in knowing your classes and therefore being in an excellent position to gauge the level of involvement and influence you should afford them. You may teach a mature and positive group who can be trusted to design a series of lessons in order to cover a whole topic, with you simply casting a watching eye over the proceedings and offering critical but constructive advice. Other groups should not be excluded from this game but might only have the power to choose from three or four options, carefully considered by you, that will form the basis of perhaps a large part of one lesson. An important aspect of this whole process is the reflection and redesign, linking back to the explicit targets that were initially set, in the same way that teachers should ponder on

CHAPTER 7 MIND GAMES

their own WWWs (what went wells) and HTIs (how to improves), with reference to particular foci, to develop their skills and effectiveness in the classroom. Where classes are especially challenging, you may have exhausted options and introducing 'student-led learning' can demonstrate your desire to work collaboratively with the group, showing trust and faith in them.

Finally, never underestimate or disregard the integrity of the young people you teach. If your questions are targeted and specific, they will give intuitive and useful feedback. So rather than asking *'What would make lessons better?'*, ask, for example, *'What types of questions can help us to better learn and remember …?'*

101 A picture to say a thousand words

'Say what you see!' If you grew up in the 1980s, that particular expression, especially when uttered in an Irish accent, brings back memories of Roy Walker hosting the TV game show *Catchphrase*. It is fairly explanatory from the name but, to clarify, contestants were presented with an image, often including the retro tech character Mr Chips, that was the clue to a (mostly) well-known phrase. The fun then ensued when wrong answers were rapidly shouted out and the patience of the presenter was tested. Everyone knows the phrase is 'half baked' and not 'cut a bake into two pieces', 'not fully baked', 'Where has the rest of the baked cake gone?' or 'I'm only half-interested in baking today'. Imagine if there were no wrong answers and any answer that demonstrated some level of relevant understanding or was loosely based on the phrase was acceptable. I am not sure how entertaining this would be on such a show, where contestant errors and stupidity are the main attraction.

However, in the classroom, the use of images to assess, review and deepen learning is both a simple and powerful win in any subject and in any topic area. Images can be used either as a starter to recap previous learning or to introduce new content or as part of a plenary that encourages students to link different aspects of learning or indeed predict the next part of the story. The challenge can be varied from an obvious image such as a mirror following a lesson on light, or (much better) a seemingly random picture to demonstrate that learning is not confined to exam specifications, textbooks or the most obvious links.

Consider, for example, a class having to link creatively a picture of an apple to their lesson on coasts, or an image of a candle burning at the end of a lesson on straight line graphs. This will take time and classes will need to be trained to offer courageous answers to such a vague question, but the excellent teacher can skilfully direct almost any student feedback to elicit key learning points or explain how a topic links to the wider world or other curriculum areas. If your students are allowed only to see learning in your classroom as separate episodes of a series, with no crossover to other aspects of their life, then their understanding and interest will always just sit on the surface of a deep and beautiful river that brims underneath with life and interconnections of which they are blissfully unaware.

CHAPTER 7 **MIND GAMES**

Mind games key takeaways

▶ Having set routines and a clear structure does provide students with safety and reliability, and gives you a useful back-up plan when needed, but being too predictable in your teaching can result in waning engagement over time. Vary your plans by starting with open questions, without sharing the learning objectives from the outset, so they do not become clear until much later in the lesson. Perhaps even ask students what they think the learning objectives are, rather than telling the class explicitly and ruining the surprise.

▶ Encourage students to take ownership and be accountable for what happens in lessons by reflecting on their role and the choices that they make. Plan for moments in lessons where you can demonstrate the improvements that they have made as a result of your teaching and their efforts. Your classroom is a place where they will enjoy (and can succeed in) their learning.

▶ Include students in your thinking and planning of learning activities, as well as the reflection and review afterwards. Demonstrate to them how they can be influenced by others through eyes-closed feedback. Although positive feedback might sometimes shield students from harsh realities, accept that there are times where it is more effective than criticism in achieving improvements (for children and adults).

▶ When asking students to follow instructions, consider the impact of the exact words that you use. Persuasive language and confident but positive body language that expects a particular response is more likely to get the desired outcome and prevent confrontation than angry or emotional demands. Use the force!

▶ Consider how you come across to your students. Build an element of mystery in your persona which can make your teaching less predictable, but at the same time increase their confidence and respect in you. Do not judge your effectiveness solely on the responses and behaviour of students. Being your own critical friend will help your wellbeing in the face of challenges and ensure that you drive your improvement.

CHAPTER 8 **FAILING, TO LEARN**

'It's fine to make mistakes – that is one of the best ways of learning'. How many of you have sat through, or indeed delivered, assemblies where we endeavour to inspire young people to pursue their goals by highlighting the struggles of figures such as James Dyson, Thomas Edison or the go-to figure of the last 20 years when it comes to overcoming setbacks as they journey onto deserved fame and recognition – JK Rowling? Do we, as teachers, practise what we preach? Maybe the more pertinent question is, are we actually allowed that luxury? Imagine responding to a complaint about our standard of teaching, classroom conduct or general professionalism by quoting the opening line of this section with a playful smile on your face and a few innocent shrugs of your shoulders, with a *'Never mind, I'll get better in time'* thrown in.

CHAPTER 8 FAILING, TO LEARN

I am of course not referring to significant safeguarding issues that draw our level of care into question – there are some 'mistakes' that are rightly never acceptable. As trainees, we should be encouraged to try different methods, be creative in our approach and just give things a go, knowing that the real teacher will pick up the pieces when we are gone. However, all of a sudden when we qualify, the stakes seem too high and the consequences of bad teaching play on our mind as we seek consistency, reliability and safety in our methods. For such a rewarding but complicated and challenging profession, is one training year really sufficient to get all our gaffes out of the way? Maybe this is why we put so much pressure on ourselves and do not broadcast the (ultimately helpful) mistakes that we make in the classroom, choosing instead to keep the door firmly shut so that others cannot witness the bedlam that all teachers will experience at times. The general approach is to gain enough skills and confidence so that you are ready to try out new ideas, while still being able to maintain control if things take an unexpected turn. However, that can leave new teachers out in the cold, looking in with envy and yearning for their training days when exploration was possible.

I would argue we need to have greater acceptance that things do go wrong in the classroom, not always but sometimes as a result of our decisions. The best teachers never stop learning as they strive to hone their skills by walking along the try-reflect-refine-retry circle.

Hopefully, I have now given sufficient justification on the need to experiment in the classroom so that when you read some of my teacher fails and you ask yourself *'Why would he try that? Surely he could see that would be a recipe for disaster'*, you might be more forgiving. Remember that necessity is the mother of invention and sometimes we are at our most creative when we have to be, but being creative does not always result in good ideas, even though our brains convince us of the logic behind these strategies and gives us the confidence to put them into practice. I am opening a vault into some stories that have not been shared with anyone, other than those very close to me. I certainly can look back and see the funny side now. Welcome to my blooper reel.

CHAPTER 8 **FAILING, TO LEARN**

The shut up circle

I really struggled with a few classes during my first years of teaching and my bad luck usually resulted in them being timetabled on the last period of the day, by which time my energy and patience gauges were dangerously close to empty, with no reserves in sight. Even though behaviour issues remained for at least a few terms, I grew fond of the students (who I could not control) within a few weeks. After all, we go into the profession to make a difference to young people, especially those who have not found positivity in education yet. Having classes that did exactly what we asked, when we asked, would lack the perverse thrill that we sought, right?

One particular Year 10 class pushed me to try one of my first teacher fails that I have never revisited – I hopped off the try-reflect ... circle pretty quickly. Even though I am going back nearly 25 years, I still vividly remember teaching that group on a Thursday afternoon. It was directly after their lunchtime, an hour's break which would sometimes result in fallings out, tears, hormonal swings and the occasional fight, leaving me to pick up the pieces and attempt to distract them with some percentages or algebra – a near impossible task. Whatever happened over lunchtime seemed to result in several students in the class needing to tell each other to *'shut up'* at the start of (or, being honest, all the way through) the lesson. My requests for them to be quiet, so that we could attempt to do some learning, were drowned out by their insults to each other. A combination of my frustration with this situation and self-confidence when it came to problem solving resulted in an idea that I convinced myself was a sure-fire winner.

The logic behind the shut up circle was linked to getting something out of your system by paying short, intense attention to it, like a scream to let out irritation. I had seen students with hyperactivity disorders managed well by being made to go for a run around the field when they presented the teacher with issues in a lesson and they would return much calmer and settle relatively peacefully into their learning. For me, the shut up circle would be the verbal equivalent of this effective method.

CHAPTER 8 FAILING, TO LEARN

The next time they entered my classroom following their lunch break and started with the insults to each other, I made the students sit in a circle and told them that for the next five minutes they would turn to the person to their right and tell them to 'shut up'. That person would not reply but instead turn to the person to their right and do the same – this would keep going around the circle until our time was up. I visualised that, at the end of the 'activity', they would return to their desks and be able to refocus on the learning, as their desire to throw out insults would be washed away and they would realise how silly their previous actions had been. This is how it would have played out in an inspirational film about teaching against the odds. I was very wrong!

Indeed, the licence that I had given them to do something they had previously done, but without my approval, only increased this behaviour but now it had become more of a joke rather than a follow on from a previous disagreement. I had to endure *'You shut up', 'No, you shut up', 'No, you shut up …'* for the remainder of the lesson. I learnt that I should not accept behaviours that fall under my expectations but how I challenge them was to be carefully considered. At the same time, I should not turn them into a game to be exploited and misinterpreted. How could I now give any sanctions out for the behaviour that I had legitimised in my classroom?

In the end, I took a better approach of discussing my thoughts on the way they treated each other, calmly, later in the lesson once the lunchtime excitement had died. This did not resolve the issue entirely but did reduce the level of the disruption and made me feel more in control.

Dictation – the relationship killer

At the start of my story, I reflected on my experiences as a student in the classroom and how, over 30 years on, I still remember those excellent teachers who inspired me and others who closed the door on a subject that otherwise could have been presented in a far more engaging way, maybe changing the direction of my life. Those memories of teachers at each end of the scale will never leave me, even if I cannot remember their names. For me, history was brought to life with the vast knowledge and confidence of my teachers. Their vivid storytelling enabled the skill of empathy to be developed, so I could understand why serfs were so unhappy in Russia in the lead up to the revolution or, despite having little interest in politics at the time, I still grasped the origins of the Chartist movement in the 1840s. In contrast, geography was delivered through dictation, lesson after lesson with very little teacher–student interaction. What an absolute waste for such an interesting and relevant subject. Therefore, when I went into teaching, I would learn from the good and never repeat the actions of the bad – or so I hoped.

It is easy to fall into bad habits, especially when they represent the path of least resistance. I am embarrassed to say that, when I felt a class had defeated me, my lessons had no real teaching but instead I often noted four points on the board; for example:
1. Copy p135
2. Do exercise 4.5
3. Copy p136
4. Do exercise 4.6.

I resigned myself to not being able to get them quiet enough to teach and therefore they would copy out (which they barely did, but at least I was not having such a public losing battle wearing me down on a regular basis). No real learning took place, as I took off my maths teacher cap and replaced it with a cover teacher one.

From that point, I killed off any chance I had with them as I demonstrated that I had no real interest in their learning or progress. I painted over the richly colourful and beautiful picture that is maths without realising (until writing this book) that I had become my old geography teacher. One of the harsh truths in teaching is that, when you start or move schools, things will be very difficult and you will have one, or a few, classes that can defeat you if you throw in the towel. However, you will come through much stronger if you battle on, showing them that you are not ready to give up on them and therefore pass the endurance test that they have obviously designed for you. My approach to this class took me a few years to recover from, as I left the school at the end of my first year there, but I never gave up on a group of students again. That was my key learning.

CHAPTER 8 **FAILING, TO LEARN**

Death by homework

You will be set homework twice a week, on Mondays and Thursdays. Each task will take you approximately 30 minutes to complete. I will not accept it if it's half done or rushed.

As we start with new classes, we aim high and set challenging, often unrealistic, expectations in order to promote the idea that we are not a teacher to be messed with. Schools will vary in their approach to homework (or better 'home learning'), but there will most likely be clear policies that inform you of the why, the how and the how much. Flexibility may exist, but only inside a small room, with four concrete walls and one tiny window. Furthermore, we convince ourselves that the best teachers set loads of homework and mark loads of homework and every student in their class always does their homework.

I felt this pressure early on in my career. We had homework booklets for each year group with tasks that needed to be completed on a weekly basis. My schedule, containing a limited amount of spare time, was carefully built around when I would mark each pile of books. I would spend about an hour on a set and then each student would spend about a minute looking at my marking – not a great ratio, really! So I'm sure that you can fully understand my frustration when sometimes a third to a half of my class did not have their homework ready by my deadline. Had I not been clear enough? Had I not been threatening enough about the consequences? Did these students not understand that doing my homework was so important? These were classes that I was already struggling with, containing many children who had other priorities outside of school and their studies – homework was quite low down on their to-do list. However, we are often not given the luxury of taking such circumstances into account because we have rules to follow and therefore 'things' that our students simply need to do. As a new teacher, I fell into the trap of upping the ante, with more and more detentions, greater lesson time spent lecturing about why classes had 'better do' what I had set and ignoring the many who had done what I had asked. The good kids were definitely not winning!

I'm sorry to say that it took me several months of losing at this game to see the light and carve a more effective path forward. When I focused on building positive relationships with classes first, centred on trust and respect, the challenge became a more manageable one. I still had the same expectations, but how I responded to non-doers changed (and as a result, fewer students were part of the *'Sorry, Sir, but I haven't done it'* club). I highlighted excellent homework much more than placing the negative in the spotlight. Staged anger and threats were pushed aside in favour of disappointment and empathy. I did not ignore the lack of effort from some and sanctions still needed to be given, but that became a minor part of my lesson, rather than dominating sections of it.

Things have moved on in the last 20 years, with peer-marked (or self-marked) tasks, research homework to encourage flipped learning and reviews of main points of previous learning. These have partly been introduced to reduce the teacher workload mountain, but also to allow for differentiated learning and to develop independence. When it comes to homework, I have learnt that there must be a clear purpose which is understood by the class, that quality is far more important than quantity and that students should be working harder than the teacher. Also, some students might rarely do homework. Although this should not be ignored, it should also not get in the way of building positive relationships, both with the individual and the class.

The 100 lines slow death, the 100 lines slow death, the 100 lines slow death ...

Imagine one aspect of your life that you consider yourself to not be very good at, or have little interest in doing – for me that would have to be DIY. Consider if (and I stress the word 'if' here) you wanted to improve in this area so sought the advice of an expert and their feedback was for you to write out, a hundred times, 'I do love doing (DIY) and will get better at it with greater motivation and effort'. How effective do you think that would be? For me, it would probably put me off the task even more, although my handwriting might improve in the short term.

Of course, we do not give students lines to copy out multiple times during a detention because we believe that the act itself will produce magical transformative outcomes. Instead, we use it as a deterrent and a stick, hoping that they will remember the boredom the next time they consider challenging your authority or not doing what was asked. I remember conversations with colleagues where we compared the lines that we gave: simple short ones were too easy to copy but could be done maybe a few hundred times, whereas those that went over a certain number of words added a few twists of the mental torture rack – teachers need to have fun too, right? For me, this is a teaching fail because it did not produce any desired improvement and actually I achieved much better results once I started engaging with students during detentions to discuss how they should behave better, or supported them with their learning so that they had more confidence and chose not to hide behind the *'I can't be bothered'* wall. I can see that using lines as an initial response may have the desired effect but when the same student is given the same punishment, you should question the rationale. Did it ever work for Bart Simpson?

The never ending story

Once I had survived my first few years in teaching and felt confident that I could maintain high standards in the classroom, I fell victim to an internal struggle. Clear rules that students needed to adhere to at the same time required flexibility where the greater good could be achieved through a conscious blurring of the lines for any individuals who would not have survived the simple game of 'right and wrong'. The concept of rules that should be followed by all, with no exceptions, creates a fair system that enables the much sought-after consistency in the classroom. Yet, there are some students who fall foul of this game and need help rather than reminders of expectations. Giving detentions for failing to do what is required is an accepted part of school life and a key factor in establishing routines and discipline, which creates a purposeful environment where all children can flourish. However, what if the student in question does not do what is required in the actual detention? Should they be given another one, perhaps elevated to a more serious sanction? When will this stop, especially if the student is unable or unwilling to change due to increased wasted time and threats, or, even worse, refuses to turn up after school? What if they really don't care or have much more important and challenging things going on in their life? Would you be happy with students receiving some form of exclusion for an initial crime of, for example, not doing enough work in a lesson?

I lived this out with one of my Year 9 top-set students. My problem really became evident when the pettiness of my actions became clear after I had travelled through a few doors of the behaviour policy, sticking to my guns. It was apparent that I would either need to back down or create a needless, but potentially significant, issue for the student, me, my head of department and the school. Relationships that win over hearts and minds are not built through a lack of care, as demonstrated by rigidness and policy quoting, but are instead born out of a genuine interest in supporting individual needs. Hence, the mental battle between clear lines defining right or wrong on one side, and shifting expectations for individuals rather than the majority on the other. Once I focused on the mutual respect that I wanted, I could see a far more positive and constructive journey ahead. The initial detention would still be given but that time would be used to discuss meaningfully, with the student, how we could work together to create improvement, through a series of smaller stepping stones. Being honest, it still did bother me that I had bent the rules, whereas others did not have this benefit. Maybe that is the mathematical logic and desire for order in me. However, I did recognise that, as the adult and the one ultimately responsible for creating and implementing solutions, I had coaxed the student onto a better path with no real disadvantage to the rest of the class.

The extra minute

Having students who present challenges almost every time you see them can be incredibly draining. Those angels who do very little work, push the boundaries of your patience with their poor attitude and then want an argument when you threaten a sanction – they are the ones that make lessons drag on, so why would you want to spend more time with them in a detention? The best (interview) answer to the question is that you can use those moments, when the rest of the class have gone, to build better understanding, and therefore improve relationships, in a one-on-one conversation that will have a positive impact on your future teaching. I would fully stand behind this concept by reflecting on a teacher fail during my first year.

CHAPTER 8 **FAILING, TO LEARN**

Being entrusted with a top-set group filled me with excitement, as I planned for having a motivated and engaged set of young people in front of me. This largely was the case but two students, who were extremely good at maths, did not seem to think that I had anything to offer them. They thought they could do better by applying minimal effort most of the time and would try a bit harder when it came to tests. After going through my standard set of techniques with no success, I reluctantly had to resort to detentions, but the problem was that the behaviour was no better during the sanction than it had been in lessons. The students again did little and still let their arrogance play out in an empty arena. I had given them a detention, so what? I could not force them to do any work. It was clear that my attempts to talk them through my expectations and ask about their motivations was a game that they were too clever to play. I had to design a new set of rules and came up with an idea that was not entirely a failure.

The next detention would be 10 minutes but every time they spoke I would add an extra minute. This is a common approach in teaching and not evidence of genius thinking, but the twist would be the humour I would bring in, hoping to give birth to some positivity, by encouraging them to speak:

'You will be here for 10 minutes, but every time you speak I will add an extra minute – do you understand?'

'Yeah.'

'OK, that is an extra minute! Do you understand?'.

'What! That's not fair!'

'That is another minute ...'

You can see how this would most likely aggravate the situation and could make things much more negative, but I smiled the second time and let them into the fun that we would have. The 11 (not 12) minutes passed enjoyably. I would ask their opinions about something and then watch them being unsure of how to respond, or ask them about their plans for the rest of the day, with something akin to a game of Simon Says, where you can never win, ensuing. I also threw in comments about the rudeness of not replying when someone has asked a question. This use of humour did end up being effective in building better relationships with those students and they did improve in lessons – so why do I consider this a fail?

Too much fun can be a bad thing as, when news of my detentions spread, others wanted to experience them and I had students asking me what they needed to do in order to be kept in by me. Unfortunately my detentions had become popular and my idea had backfired to a certain extent, but my reputation for being an 'OK' teacher was enhanced. I had learnt that reminding students that you are the one in control can be achieved through some alternative and jovial ways when the go-to strategies fall flat.

Sarcastic lack of wit

Humour is a key part of the excellent teacher's armour, but who decides what is and what is not funny? As Oscar Wilde proclaimed, sarcasm is the lowest form of wit but the highest form of intelligence. However, sarcasm can also be a rather obvious vehicle to demonstrate frustrations, disappointment or general negativity, and teachers should be careful about how their perceived satire may come across to others. I have always considered myself to have a decent level of dry wit and have learnt how to apply this effectively in lessons, but I hit a few stumbling blocks along the way.

Before I get into detail, let me reflect on my current role, which sometimes involves dealing with student or parent complaints about teachers. Often there is a desire from the aggrieved party to enhance the reference to a specific incident or lesson, with more general points about how a teacher usually treats their class (unless they are being observed). Unkind comments, badly disguised as attempts at humour, at the expense of individuals is a fairly common statement when 'evidence' is presented. Does that mean that teachers should be careful when trying to add light humour into their lessons? Not really, although it entirely depends on the relationship that the teacher has built with a class. Groups who believe that a teacher likes them and is 'on their side' will be much more lenient when attempts at comedy result in a faux pas and laughter from students is replaced with quizzical stares. However, in the absence of a positive connection

CHAPTER 8 **FAILING, TO LEARN**

with a class, statements such as *'I really, really enjoy teaching you, especially on a Friday afternoon. Probably the highlight of my whole week'* or *'The work that you produced this lesson is truly inspirational. I think I will frame some of it and put it up on my living room wall at home. It is just a blank space at the moment so it would not really be too different'* and *'Oh yes, of course you are all capable of a grade 5 or higher – have any of you considered Oxford or Cambridge? Only for the shopping, I was not talking about university!'* are probably best avoided.

I certainly resorted to such tactics early in my career, when I found a class particularly challenging and I was exploring ways to try to get them to see my side. Did this improve their behaviour? Not really, it just showcased my frustration and my lack of skill in developing strategies, and firmly established who held the reins of power, thus delaying the eventual slow progress that I would make with them.

Earlier, we discussed avoiding telling a class that they were the worst you have ever taught. Using sarcasm to vent annoyance is equally ineffective in gaining any respect or giving you any credibility as a teacher.

The 'I've totally lost it' yell

When starting teaching and being in front of classes several times a day, many of us will go from using our voice very little, in our day-to-day lives, to a profession where it is the primary tool in your job. As we learn to 'talk the talk', we explore different approaches, from the quiet comforting 'mouse' voice, the firm deliberate deep voice and the loud thunderous boom shout. Each has its place and can be effective when used in the appropriate scenario. However, the king of kings in getting immediate quiet, when we begin our career, is the yell. You can give it all you have and the stunned silence that follows has to be taken advantage of. There is a peculiar sense of achievement and pride that you can actually create the classroom tranquillity that you so crave, when all other methods have failed. However, of course this is a forced and short-term gain, not one that has much sustainability.

As you observe and learn about the excellent teachers in your school, ask yourself why they rarely need to raise their voice and certainly don't yell in an uncontrollable and crazed manner. Unfortunately, new teachers do not have the luxury of experience and I certainly resorted to the yell fairly quickly with many of my classes: *'I have told you to be quiet three times. Now will you just shut up so that I can teach!'* (possibly with a please thrown in there somewhere) or *'I have tried and tried and tried with you lot and I am telling you now that if you do not stop talking and start listening, then there will be trouble. I am not joking, try me!'*. The issue that arose, for me as a new teacher, is that I now had to follow up my bold statement, but by using up so much energy my mind had gone blank and, as I stared at the class staring back at me, the moment was gone and the noise returned. I lost my voice within a few months of starting and rallied on, semi-heroically, being forced to develop much better methods of talking and winning over a group. I never looked back. I cannot remember the last time I deployed the uncontrolled shout: the 'I've totally lost it yell' is somewhere catching dust, hopefully never to be seen again.

Honeymoon? What honeymoon?

Sometimes moving to a new school can be harder than when you start in your first role as a teacher. There is much to be said for finding the right place, where you feel a deep sense of belonging and loyalty. However, dark forces can push you towards promotion and convince you that, once you have established yourself, you can stroll into any new environment that might, from the outside, look like a similar school. But all schools are different and similar intakes or results only tell a small portion of the story, as I found out. Having built a good level of confidence from my first four years of teaching, I was ready for the next challenge and the increased responsibility that I was told I should be taking on – the natural stepping stone of a second in department position.

Even looking back now, I do not feel that I was complacent in any way, as I had been mentally walking through my first lesson with each group. I would use those initial weeks, when students are trying to figure out their new teacher, to establish myself in a calm and assured manner. I had been through this before and would use my experience to win over my new classes. My mistake was to assume that I would

CHAPTER 8 **FAILING, TO LEARN**

have the luxury of a honeymoon period. Surely this is a right of every teacher when teaching a new class or starting in a new school? Apparently not.

My day from hell, where I would see my new Year 10 and Year 11 classes, came straight after a pleasant inset day where I was introduced and welcomed to the school. I had been given a top set in Year 11 but had not been warned that one of the students had recently been spiralling out of control, in and out of school. My *'I am Mr Singh and this is what I expect'* speech was going OK but then the student, who was sitting at the front, got a football out of his bag and proceeded to bounce it on the floor while staring straight at me. I gave a simple response of *'Can you stop doing that, please? Thank you'* but he just continued with no change in his demeanour. I tried again but had no effect, with the rest of the class enjoying the show with a mix of sympathy for me and bemusement that I was letting this go. I was obviously irritated but had to remain calm so I finished my introduction and decided I would speak to this student at the end of the lesson. That never happened as he simply walked off, ignoring my pleas for him to remain. I had certainly not expected this type of honeymoon. However, the worst was yet to come in the afternoon when I saw my bottom Year 10 set.

I had a small group of about 15 students, who mostly walked into the room as if I was not there and proceeded to chat, using extremely choice language about their most recent exploits. Eventually, I managed to get them to sit down and, as I was starting my rehearsed 'welcome', the students (maybe not all but definitely most) started banging on their desks and chanting loudly. I had never faced this type of behaviour before and had to think quickly. Again, I opted for a calm approach and waited for their energy to die down, which took several minutes, before I questioned their reasoning for such behaviour in a hope to demonstrate to them that I would not be provoked into an angry reaction. However, they seemed to take that as an invite to restart – this continued for most of the lesson. I learnt, the following day, that a nearby teacher made a complaint about me (or my class), which resulted in a meeting to discuss my actions, ability and professionalism in my first week at the school. Not the start I had hoped for.

Patience and calmness are a great asset to any teacher, but in the wrong situation can be perceived as a weakness. These incidents were among my most significant teacher fails and taught me about the need to impose yourself on classes immediately, in a composed manner if the situation allows. If that is not the case, use more forceful means and if neither of these work then follow the school policy on how to deal with disruptive students, seeking help from nearby experienced colleagues without delay.

Names on the board – the naughty list

There are some classroom methods that schools encourage or that colleagues swear by, which might be effective for many teachers but have never made it into my tried-and-tested collection of strategies. This is mainly due to my lack of faith and therefore lack of persistence with them. However, as a new teacher, I was willing to give almost anything a go. The clear and simple rationale here seems logical. If you have a small number of students in a class who are not meeting your expectations then write their names on the board and, at the end of the lesson, those on the 'naughty list' will need to face some type of sanction. I hesitantly decided to give this a go with one of my first classes, a lively Year 9 group, which I was struggling with. I laid out the rules for this new game, explaining to the class that I was tired of the behaviour of a few individuals disrupting the learning of the majority who were keen to get on and do well.

There was some initial success, with the group responding more positively in the classroom, but after the first few lessons it became clear that getting your name on the board was seen as a welcome challenge by a few students as it gave them the visible attention that they craved – at the front of the classroom for all to see. I would spend the lesson being more focused on who needed to be added to the list than teaching, and some in the class wanted to dispute or discuss the merits of adding one name over another. The fact that they would receive some type of detention or speaking to did not seem to be a major deterrent and was actually no different to how I had been dealing with them previously. The change was the increased notoriety being gifted to them that totally went against my principle of 'letting the good kids win'. I abandoned the method after a few weeks and looking back was never really behind the idea so it was probably doomed from the start.

CHAPTER 8 FAILING, TO LEARN

To help my teaching, I learnt that improving the behaviour of individuals in classes is best done through building positive relationships and not by adding more stipulations that individuals could seek to exploit. I have seen excellent teachers using a 'good names' list on the board to acknowledge and reward positive behaviour and effort, and therefore demonstrate that attention is readily available for those who impress rather than disrupt. To be honest, there are already plenty of strategies in place in most classrooms for students who misbehave. Find the few that are most effective for you but avoid any that indirectly reward those in your firing line.

Too much fun

'Sir, it is our last lesson of the year, can we have a fun lesson?' Most teachers will be familiar with this phrase, spoken by the innocent, wide-eyed, hopeful little angels that fill our classes. After a few years of teaching, I developed some witty (only in my opinion) but unhelpful responses, such as *'All my lessons are fun!', 'Maths is fun'* or *'Yes, you are right, let's do some simultaneous equations'*. However, many teachers are drawn into this clever ruse and affected by guilt, which results in the planning of a 'fun quiz'. What possibly could go wrong?

Before I share my story, let us take a step back and consider the rationale of this decision. At the end of term, both teachers and students are tired and, as a result, patience is running low, with the ability to make good decisions waning. Throwing in an element of unhealthy competition and topping it off with the ultimate prize (a bag of sweets) and the simple recipe for a disaster is created. As a slow learner, it took me several attempts to pull off the nearly impossible task of running a well-managed, civilised, fun quiz before I realised that a different approach was required. My end-of-term lessons would usually end in disagreements between students, with verbal and physical exchanges, emotional accusations of cheating and attempts to steal the prize, along with me trying unsuccessfully to control the mayhem that I had inadvertently created. Then my unhappy class was passed onto their next teacher, who then had to suffer as a result.

Of course, we want our students to enjoy lessons and there is absolutely nothing wrong with ending on a high as we wave them off for the summer but, for early career teachers, this can be a fine line to walk when fatigue alters behaviours – theirs and yours. Setting up ground rules and expectations, creating a winning situation for all students and limiting the potential for feelings of unfairness can all help to create the right environment where everyone can enjoy the 'fun'. Alternatively, follow the guidance of many school leaders who ask for normality in the last few days of term, with a hope that behaviour issues can be kept to a minimum. In addition, why not plan for 'fun' activities throughout the year as part of regular teaching? Then your students can learn from experience how to better manage such situations.

Finally, if you are not convinced that these types of lessons will help your teaching, then carefully check your contract to see whether having fun quizzes at the end of term is a requirement of your role. Students might try to convince you that you are the only teacher who will not play the game, but this is most likely far removed from the truth.

The helpful, unhelpful, suspiciously super-slow, resources hander outer

There are certain phrases that a teacher might say which will result in a sea of hands being raised, especially with younger classes, such as *'I need a volunteer'*. As we get older, we respond to such requests with deep suspicion until we know what the task entails. In contrast, it seems that our students will happily sign up for the unknown, probably thinking it will get them out of doing work or perhaps placing trust in the kindness of their teacher. Gone, I hope, are the days of (science) teachers amusing themselves by asking students to request a 'long stand' or 'long weight' from one of their colleagues. Instead, giving out books or handing out resources seems to be a task that some students cannot help but put themselves forward for. The job specification is quite simple: collect the items and then hand them out. Training is not required. However, in the wrong hands, this role provides an opportunity to disrupt the calm environment you have created or to slow down the pace of your lesson. I have certainly been taken advantage of by students who have exploited the brief freedom which they have been afforded.

In my first few years, I remember advice from a head of year to use a student, who had poor behaviour and motivation in my lessons, to help

CHAPTER 8 **FAILING, TO LEARN**

with giving out and taking in resources. I suppose that they felt more valued in my lessons with their new responsibility, but it just gave them greater scope to disrupt, maybe due to my lack of careful planning and consideration of a strategy which I considered to be extremely simple. With the exception of practical lessons, where perhaps the careful management of equipment requires student helpers, I do not see the need for 'volunteers' in this area. Learning from my experiences, I now always distribute resources by placing them at the end of desks and ask the class to pass them along, without needing to stand up or walk around. The same can be done when collecting them back. *'Pass your textbooks along each row. Can the one at the end of the row make a tidy pile and then I will collect them back in'.* I have not looked back with this simple win.

Oggy oggy oggy, oi oi oi

When I completed my PGCE at the age of 22, I secretly doubted that I was ready to work with young people, still feeling that I was one myself. I had never volunteered to help out with clubs for children (such as Cubs or sports teams). I felt that I had minimal teaching experience from my training year, including those two long weeks of observations before starting my course – one at a primary school and one at my old secondary school. Quite rightly, one of the key aspects of the current application process for teacher training courses is the requirement for experience of working with children in educational and other areas. This allows you to witness firsthand the challenges and rewards on offer and you can therefore decide, from an informed position, if you are brave enough to pursue this career. I would argue that it is much easier to learn how to engage, motivate and teach young people within the formal setting of a school environment than in outdoor extracurricular activities, where excitement is sometimes difficult to contain. The teaching fail that follows is not one of my own; however, it has certainly left its mark on me and resulted in shaping my approach when I would go on to lead school sports teams.

Most teachers who have experienced the pleasure (or indeed torture) of attending residential team-building trips with companies such as PGL (short for 'Parents Get Lost', I believe) can possibly predict the rest of this section. Picture taking away a whole Year 7 group of nearly 200 students, accompanied by 15 to 20 staff, on a week-long trip full of fun and excitement. Their day is filled with outdoor activities, such as abseiling or problem solving, that test students' individual and collective skills, away from the comfort of their electronic devices. The key to the success of these activities is the competency of the instructor and the effectiveness of their training on working productively with young people in an environment far removed from schools and classrooms. Achieving the right balance between encouraging excitement and being aware of key safety issues can be difficult, especially if the instructors are in their late teens and taking on this possibly low-paid role is one of their first stepping stones since leaving school.

So, now the scene has been set and we have a group of 15 exuberant youngsters being led by an 18 year old whose training seems to have revolved around loud chants and irritatingly repetitive songs. *'Guys, when I say "oggy, oggy oggy", you shout "oi, oi, oi". Then we get quiet because I have some safety instructions that you need to listen to. OK? Here we go. OGGY, OGGY, OGGY!'* The painfully loud reply is heard far and wide: *'OI, OI, OI!'*. As I am sure you can imagine, this was often not followed by the required golden silence which would enable safety protocols to be shared, but instead laughter and conversations that left the instructor looking bemused, as this was clearly not what they asked for. The same pattern followed throughout an exhausting week where I and other staff had to deal with complaints about how our students were far too loud and did not listen, with some activities needing to be abandoned as a result. Whose failure was this? The instructors? Their trainers? The school? The students? Everyone can share in some responsibility but a simple message which I passed onto the deaf ears of the lead instructors was: if you want young people to be quiet then don't get them to chant or sing beforehand.

Attending a residential trip like this should be a must for any new teacher. It will enhance their skills by observing others in a different environment and those important moments of learning can definitely have applications in the classroom.

The Singh bin

After about five years of teaching, I became very confident in my ability to achieve decent behaviour with my classes and this was

CHAPTER 8 FAILING, TO LEARN

further confirmed when 'naughty' students from other groups would sometimes be sent to sit at the back of my room. By this stage, my teaching of difficult groups would centre on rigid formality, with silent starter activities followed by a short discussion and then whiteboard teaching resulting in textbook work. It was not especially inspirational but it provided a structure that reduced behaviour issues and was clearly evident to colleagues who would walk into my lessons.

The challenging and lonely life of a teacher often results in the strong urge to support those who we work with and the flexibility due to the setting of classes can be a luxury for maths teachers, enabling students to move between classes. Therefore when, during a department meeting, we discussed an especially testing year group, I volunteered to take certain students into my class and swap them out with more engaged ones. And so the Singh Bin was born – not a formal term or one that I ever shared with the group, but just one which sat in my mind. The logic and rationale was not flawed, but my execution was a key learning point for me.

I continued with the same format of lessons, but clearly this was harder with students of differing abilities so the work set had to be flexible, which meant that the rigid structure was eroded. However, my main mistake was to not address the set changes in a positive way by welcoming my new students into my classroom. It was pretty obvious to them what had happened; the bad kids are being moved to Mr Singh and the good ones are in the other groups – young people are incredibly astute. The Singh Bin became more and more apathetic and although behaviour was not a huge issue, spirit and energy was absent and students were even less motivated and therefore little work was done.

All young people need to feel valued and confident that their teacher enjoys having them in their lessons and will not give up on them, whatever behaviours they may demonstrate. On reflection, this had the potential for being a real positive in their learning and development. I could have given a speech about how much I wanted them in my lessons, as I knew deep down that they had much more to offer than they were currently demonstrating and, together, we could show this to the whole school. Actually, this would have not been so far from the truth.

CHAPTER 9 **THE PLENARY – THE END OF THE BEGINNING**

My story, which I have shared with you in bitesize chunks, is not so remarkable. We enter the profession with selflessness and a moral purpose, whether we are born to be teachers walking down the path laid out before us, or whether we stumble unwittingly into it, our destiny hidden from us until the secret door is opened. We are unfazed by the challenges that lie ahead, often with some naivety, not fully appreciating the length of the twisting tunnel which has to be navigated before we can bathe in the light at the other end. Positivity is our armour, personality is our weapon, with our ability to learn from mistakes and adapt quickly acting as our supply of ammunition. Our training is carefully managed by battle-hardened experts in a series of staged but almost realistic drills, so that we build confidence and begin to wonder what all the fuss was about. *Wasn't teaching supposed*

CHAPTER 9 THE PLENARY – The End of the Beginning

to be difficult? Even when we are told about the great leap from the protection of the training year to our start as a real teacher, with our own classes and intense timetable, we have been brainwashed into believing that we are more than ready. Then we suffer our first defeat against the class that simply will not do what is asked. The battle is so one-sided that we wonder if we were involved at all or whether we ever had a chance. Imposter syndrome rears its ugly head. However, we have other classes that rebuild our self-belief and confirm that this is the right path for us. Further thinking allows us to build determination, as we regroup against our nemesis and face failure head on.

The first few years of teaching are the most difficult – **this cannot be stressed enough**. Planning numerous lessons for a full teaching week, meeting deadlines for reports, being asked for immediate, detailed feedback on students, being a form tutor, marking work, responding to parents, as well as something else which escapes my mind right now … ah yes, actually teaching! Having to deliver four or five hours of lessons each day is an incredibly exhausting task, both physically and mentally, even if you are enjoying a honeymoon period. Mistakes will undoubtedly be made, but you do not have the luxury of time to lick your wounds and regroup, as your next class is at the door ready to test your skills. You reach the end of the week and face the weekend dilemma of whether to have the rest that you sorely need or to spend time planning for the lessons ahead, so that you do not fall behind so early in the term. One week merges into the next and the conveyor belt moves onwards with stops and starts, some obvious and others unexpected, ensuring that you stay alert. Then, strangely enough, the difficult and draining journey becomes more enjoyable, with a real sense of achievement as that conveyor belt stops and you crawl towards the promised land of the half term 'break'. Your health points are regained and you start again, with your determination to teach better lessons giving you renewed energy and focus. Before you know it, the year has flown by and you have earned the 'I survived my first year in teaching' t-shirt. It is easy to simply recognise the fact that you have improved without considering the how or why. You are building your own library of simple wins, but this fact may not be obvious to you at this stage. You **are** becoming a good teacher and that is the most important thought to dwell on.

CHAPTER 9 THE PLENARY – The End of the Beginning

Teaching cannot be conquered with a paint-by-numbers approach and simple wins unfortunately do not work all the time. Within the complexities of educating young people, there are no guarantees and often no logical reasoning explaining why a seemingly flawed strategy is bizarrely effective or why the most sensible approach does not give the (predicted) desired results.

This is not a recipe book where you can refer to particular sections when the situation dictates a required course of action, ensuring that you have the ingredients you need at your fingertips. I do not have all the answers, I might not even have most of them and actually your questions might differ from the ones that I am aiming to address. I have tried to cover the key areas, given my experience in teaching and knowing that after 25 years I continue to learn, fail and succeed, but most importantly try, immensely enjoying the whole process and relishing playing the game more and more.

Your journey and story will differ from mine. Just as all children are unique, teaching cannot be uniform and is not so straightforward that it can be programmed or injected into willing participants. However, there will be similarities and common challenges that we will all face and I hope that some of my wins and failures will resonate enough to assist you along the way, as you venture into the greatest series of adventures that make up the life of a teacher. You have reached the end of the beginning when you have mastered the basics of behaviour management. Now you are ready to craft and deliver inspiring and enjoyable lessons. Be humble, but also allow yourself some confidence.

Most importantly, remember that when the teacher, full of noble intentions, wins, everyone wins.

www.ingramcontent.com/pod-product-compliance
Lightning Source LLC
Chambersburg PA
CBHW062226080426
42734CB00010B/2040